The test of the goodness of a thing is its fitness for use. If it fails on this first test, no amount of ornamentation or finish will make it any better; it will only make it more expensive, more foolish. Frank Pick, 1916

RICHARD TAYLOR

EDWARD JOHNSTON

A SIGNATURE FOR LONDON

UNICORN

in association with

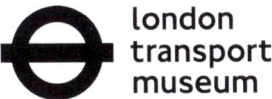

First published by Unicorn,
an imprint of the Unicorn Publishing Group LLP, 2016

101 Wardour Street
London
W1F 0UG

www.unicornpublishing.org

The moral right of the author has been asserted

Text © London Transport Museum

All rights reserved. No part of this publication may be reproduced, stored in or introduced into a retrieval system, or transmitted, in any form or by any means (electronic, mechanical, photocopying, recording or otherwise), without the prior written permission of the copyright holders and the above publisher of this book.

The publisher has made every effort to contact the current copyright holders of the pictures included in this book. Any omission is unintentional, and relevant information should be addressed to the Unicorn Publishing Group to be included in any reprint.

ISBN 978 1 910787 29 8

The roundel logo is the trade mark of Transport for London (TfL)

Many of the images reproduced in this book are from the London Transport Museum collection, © TfL. Sources for all other images are as follows: Central St Martins Museum and Study Collection, page 32; Ditchling Museum Collection, pages 6, 15, 31, 41 and 96; private collections: pages 12, 13, 18 (both), 19, 20, 27 (both), 28, 29, 34, 35, 36, 37, 38, 39 (both), 41, 55, 70 (three on right).

Designed by Webb and Webb Design Limited
Edited and indexed by Cameron & Hollis

Printed in Slovenia

CONTENTS

FOREWORD BY SAM MULLINS	7
INTRODUCTION	11
A CRAFTSMAN'S LIFE	21
JOHNSTON AND LONDON	45
POSTSCRIPT: JOHNSTON AFTER JOHNSTON	69
NOTES	81
BIBLIOGRAPHY	88
INDEX	91
AUTHOR'S ACKNOWLEDGEMENTS	95

Let me not to the marriage of true mindes
Admit impediments, loue is not loue
Which alters when it alteration findes,
Or bends with the remouer to remoue.
O no, it is an euer fixed marke
That lookes on tempests and is neuer shaken;
It is the star to euery wandring barke
Whose worths vnknowne, although his higth be taken.
Lou's not Times foole, though rosie lips and cheeks
Within his bending sickles compasse come,
Loue alters not with his breefe houres and weekes,
But beares it out euen to the edge of doome:
If this be error and vpon me proued,
I neuer writ, nor no man euer loued.

Shakespeares Sonnet 116, from the Doves Press edition (1909) following the 1st printed edn. (of 1609); But the long ʃs are reintroduced, & the marking of the quatrains introduced, by E.J. who has written this for Mary Ginnett for S. Elizabeth's day 1927. Ɛuanst. 18.19.N.1927.A.D.

FOREWORD

How did Edward Johnston, an enthusiast for medieval manuscript illumination, come to design the typeface and logo of the most progressive urban transport organisation in the world? The circle-and-bar TfL roundel is today one of the world's most recognised brands, a beacon for that indispensable asset of a civilised city: London's integrated transport system. Encountered at the entrance to an Underground station, on a poster, a bus, tram, hire bike, bus stop or pier, it is as redolent of everyday journeys in the capital as the ubiquitous public announcements on the Underground system: 'mind the gap', 'please have your ticket ready at the barrier', 'pass right down the car please'.

Frank Pick, the Commercial Director of the Underground Group, commissioned Johnston to design a new letterform for the system, aiming for what we would today describe as a brand strategy for public transport in London. Pick wanted something to match and express his vision of 'the metropolis as a centre of life, of civilisation more intense, more eager, more vitalising than has ever so far obtained', and in 1916 Johnston delivered his 'Standard Alphabet', soon to become known as Johnston Sans.[1]

The Johnston Sans or Underground typeface was followed by the 'bullseye' or roundel and together these became the building blocks of the London Underground brand. That Edward Johnston's work for the Underground has stood the test of time so magnificently is remarkable: his designs have survived significant corporate changes, the inevitable vagaries of fashion and style, and, most recently, digital reincarnation. Johnston's legacy is now so pervasive that it is indisputably part of the city's identity, serving as branding for London itself.

Shakespeare's Sonnet 116, calligraphy in brown and red inks on vellum by Edward Johnston, made in 1927 for Mary Ginnett, daughter of Louis Ginnett, one of the artists living in the Ditchling community. The style, chosen by Johnston to slow down the reader's eye, is based on that of 14th-century English writing.

London Transport Museum is delighted to mark the centenary of Edward Johnston's first commission for the Underground with the publication of this account by Richard Taylor which covers both Johnston the man and Johnston the lettering specialist and analyses how Johnston Sans and the roundel developed over the decades. Richard Taylor was the first curator of 'Johnston Journeys', a project (generously funded by the Heritage Lottery Fund) set up to re-examine the collections of the London Transport Museum, allowing new insights into Johnston's contributions to graphic design. Here he provides an illuminating account of how an enduring alphabet for London was created by a man whose work uniquely bridged the Arts & Crafts Movement and modern industrial design.

Sam Mullins
Director, London Transport Museum

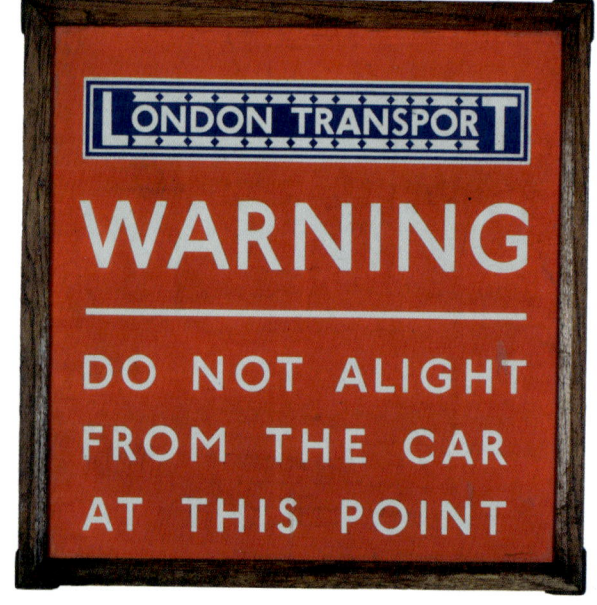

Post-1945 adaptation of the Johnston ribboned logo. The original Underground was replaced by London Transport as this was felt to be more representative of the entire corporation.

Opposite Station man Eric England clearing snow on the platform at Finchley East, 1962.

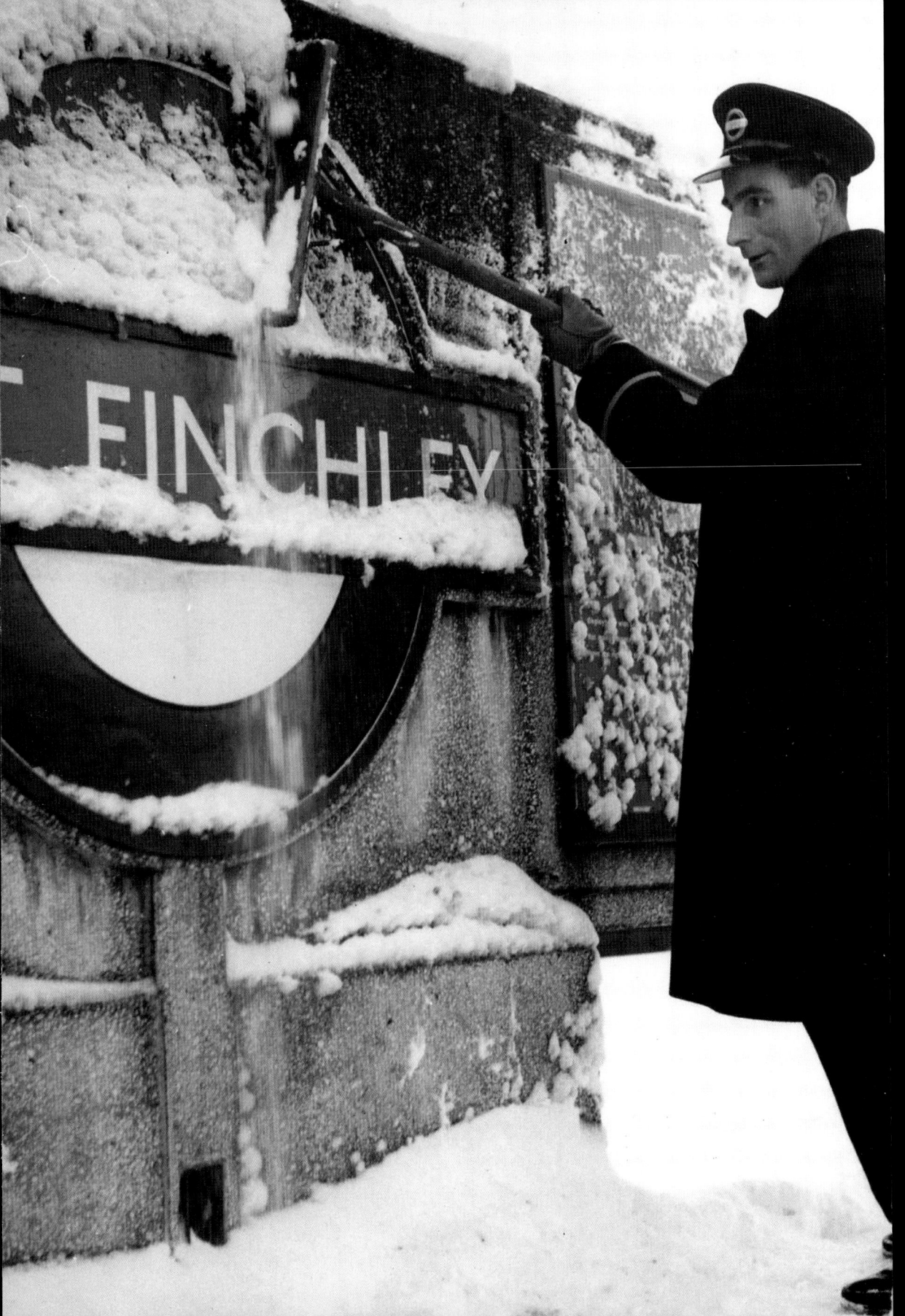

14 Line
2¼ inch
CAPS
ONLY

ABCDEFGHIJ
KLMNOPQRS
TUVWXYZ
,.:;-'!?&
1234567890

16 Line
2⅝ inch
CAPS
ONLY

ABCDEFGHIJ
KLMNOPQR
STUVWXYZ
,.:'-!?&
1234567890

INTRODUCTION

The test of the goodness of a thing is its fitness for use. If it fails on this first test, no amount of ornamentation or finish will make it any better; it will only make it more expensive, more foolish. Frank Pick, 1916 [2]

The Johnston Underground 'sans serif' was the greatest single practical contribution that has been made to 'good printing' in the last thirty years … Its standardisation on the Underground conferred upon it, as lettering, a sanction, civic and commercial, such as had not been accorded to an alphabet since the time of Charlemagne. Stanley Morison, 1947 [3]

Edward Johnston's Standard Alphabet and his bar-and-circle 'bullseye' logotype designed in 1916 for the Underground Electric Railways of London (UERL) are a remarkable expression of the profound influence of the late-19th-century Arts and Crafts Movement. They also epitomise one of the most important British modernist projects of the early 20th century: the creation and branding of London's transport network as a single identifiable entity. The resilience and adaptability of Johnston's designs over a century of change make them the ultimate expression of Frank Pick's adherence to the principle of 'fitness for purpose' as well as a reminder of the original meaning of that now rather over-used phrase.

Priscilla Johnston, Edward Johnston's daughter, relates that, when composing his *Who's Who* entry in 1937 he described his three main life achievements as follows:

Reference sheet of Johnston Sans printed by Waterlows (UERL's preferred printer) to be sent out to signwriters, mid 1920s to 1930s.

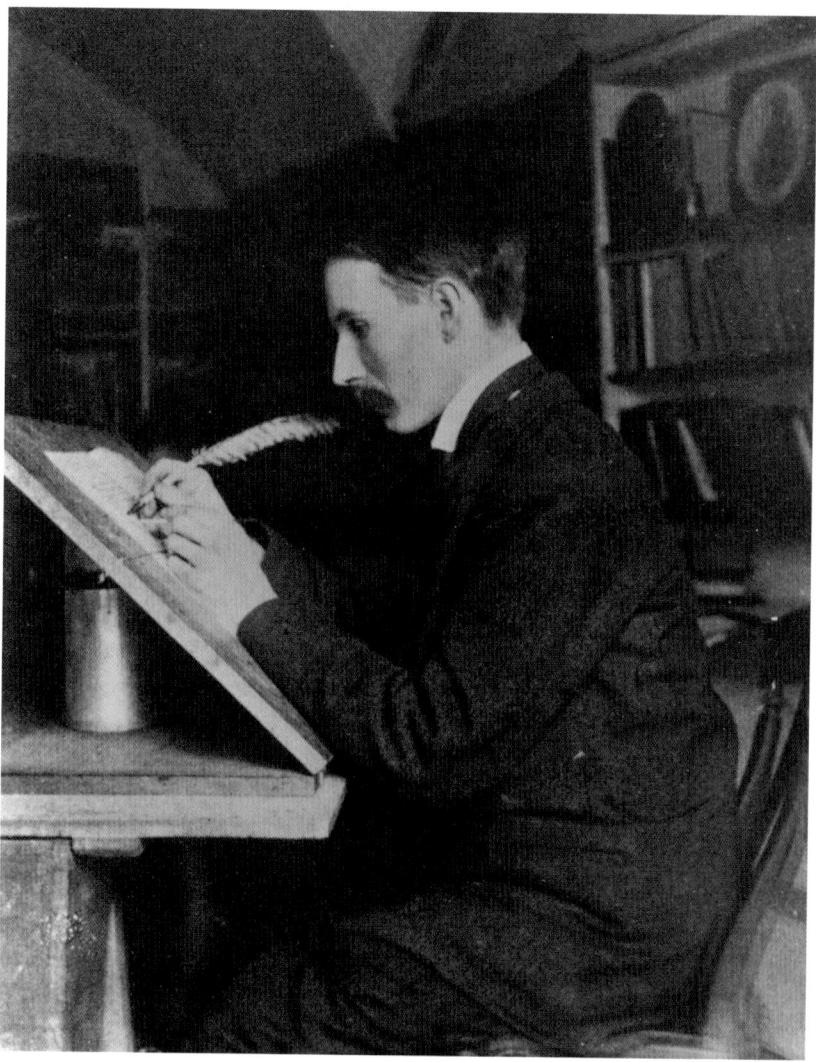

Edward Johnston at his desk in Lincoln's Inn, London, 1902.

'Studied pen shapes of letters in early MSS, British Museum ... Teacher of the first classes in formal penmanship and lettering ... and designed block lettering based on classical Roman capital proportions (for London Electric Railways).' [4]

In his covering letter to the editor, Johnston requested that his exact 'unconventional' wording be retained, adding that mentioning the block lettering would be 'pointless' without a reference to what had inspired it.

INTRODUCTION

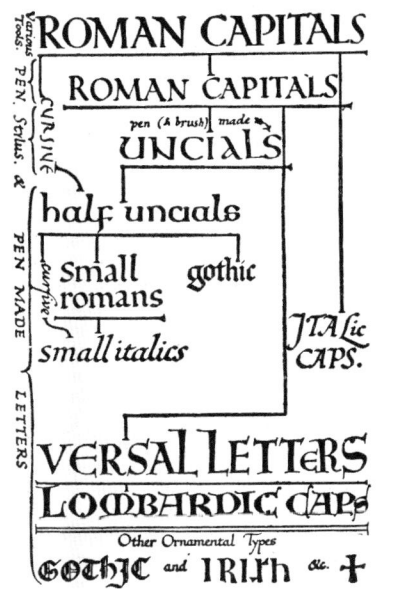
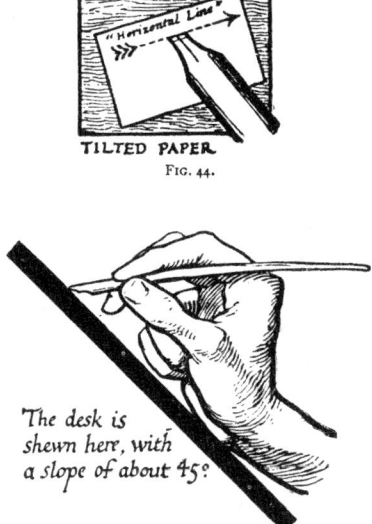

'Pen made letters' and 'Holding the pen'. Illustrations from Edward Johnston's *Writing & Illuminating & Lettering*, 1906

In both his life and his work Edward Johnston embodied a (perhaps rather British) conservative modernism: practicality, logical thinking and a belief in social benefit (in an urban context) were yoked in creative tension with the romantic ideal of the independent, self-sufficient craft worker producing handmade items, preferably in a rural setting. Stanley Morison's tribute (quoted on page 11) is perhaps the best-known articulation of the reverence that Johnston inspired in following generations. By contrast, the criticisms voiced (c.1935) by William Graily Hewitt, one of Johnston's pupils but also his near-contemporary, are a useful reminder that his work was not universally admired: 'Despite all [Johnston] did for us … he has undone too much by forsaking his standard of the classical Roman Alphabet – giving the world, without safeguard of explanation, his block letters which disfigure our modern life. His prestige has obscured their vulgarity and commercialism.'[5]

Johnston, for his part, 'acknowledged the tensions, but without becoming precious about them'.[6] The revival of the craft of formal calligraphy at the turn of the 20th century is almost entirely ascribable to Johnston, first as autodidact, then as a teacher and writer. His seminal 1906 work, *Writing & Illuminating & Lettering*, is a classic manual of craft practice which, with Johnston's later revisions, has remained a useful work of reference ever since. Peter Holliday, in his magisterial study published in 2007, sets out how Johnston's revival of hand-drawn lettering drew on William Morris's earlier experiments in calligraphy and was founded squarely on an Arts and Crafts mentality. In this worldview, the mass-produced steel nib pen, the copperplate engraver's pointed burin and – horror of horrors – the typewriter were all seen as degenerative influences on the practice of formal handwriting.[7]

Having inspected ancient Roman letter forms such as those inscribed on Trajan's Column, Johnston rediscovered, through close study of manuscripts in the British Museum Library, the mediaeval scribe's broad-edged pen. This tool, 'rightly handled', allowed him to develop (for his teaching) a 'foundational hand', a style of lettering consisting in 'essential forms of letters beautiful in themselves', based on his interpretation of the 10th-century Ramsey Psalter.[8]

Johnston's intention, clearly expressed throughout this life in his calligraphic manuscripts, was to work truthfully with the materials and, as Peter Holliday has put it, 'without empty mimicry and foolish affectations'.[9] Priscilla Johnston's view was that he was never able to come to terms with the idea of craftsmen designing for industry. When resigning as President of the Arts and Crafts Exhibition Society in 1936, she relates, his parting message was that 'he knew – and detested – the way that the craftsman's design would be blunted and coarsened in the process of mass-production.' That same year he refused for the second time to allow himself to be nominated by the Royal Society of Arts as a Registered Designer for Industry 'because "INDUSTRY" does not appear to be based on good principles or to be aimed at good purpose.'[10]

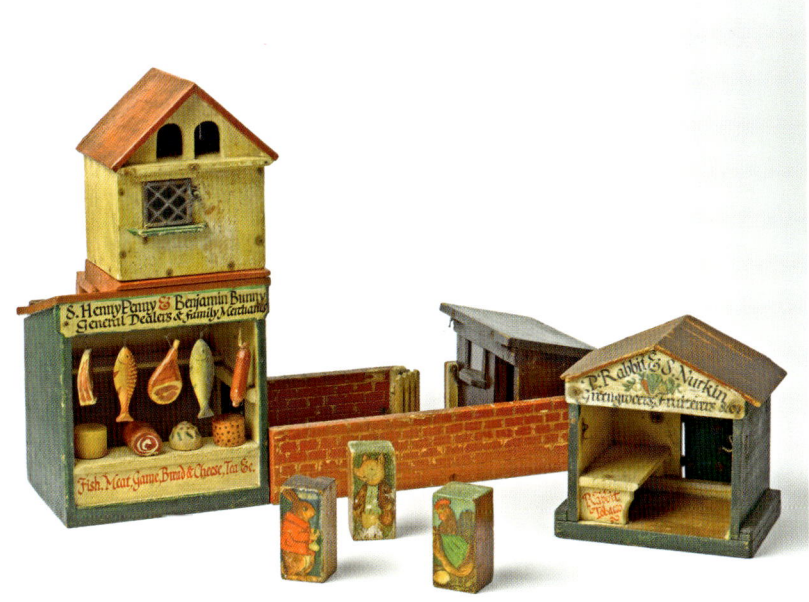

Two toy shops and a pigsty made from painted wood and metal, c.1914; in the foreground are play blocks painted with anthropomorphised animals, known as 'puk-wudgies' by the family. One of Johnston's daughters, Priscilla, wrote that 'his toys were as near perfection as he could make them.'

And yet, as Holliday observes, whereas Morris's approach to calligraphy was 'passionate but individualistic' Johnston's was 'passionate and analytical'.[11] Johnston's deep-rooted respect for the skills of the hand craftsman was a defining characteristic, but so too were a rigorously analytical approach and an ability to deconstruct problems. When he was a boy, Johnston's interests ranged across the arts and sciences. He was an avid reader of the popular science magazine *The Aerial World* and an inveterate tinkerer and constructor of mechanical and electrical gadgets as well as intricately constructed toys and games for his sisters and later his daughters.[12] In his later work on transport lettering this mechanical aptitude revealed itself in his use of algebra to calculate the proportions for his condensed alphabets for the London General Omnibus Company (1919) and his bold sans-serif block letters for the Underground (1927).

The aim of the Arts and Crafts Movement was, as Bernard Newdigate put it, 'not so much to encourage the production of

EDWARD JOHNSTON – A SIGNATURE FOR LONDON

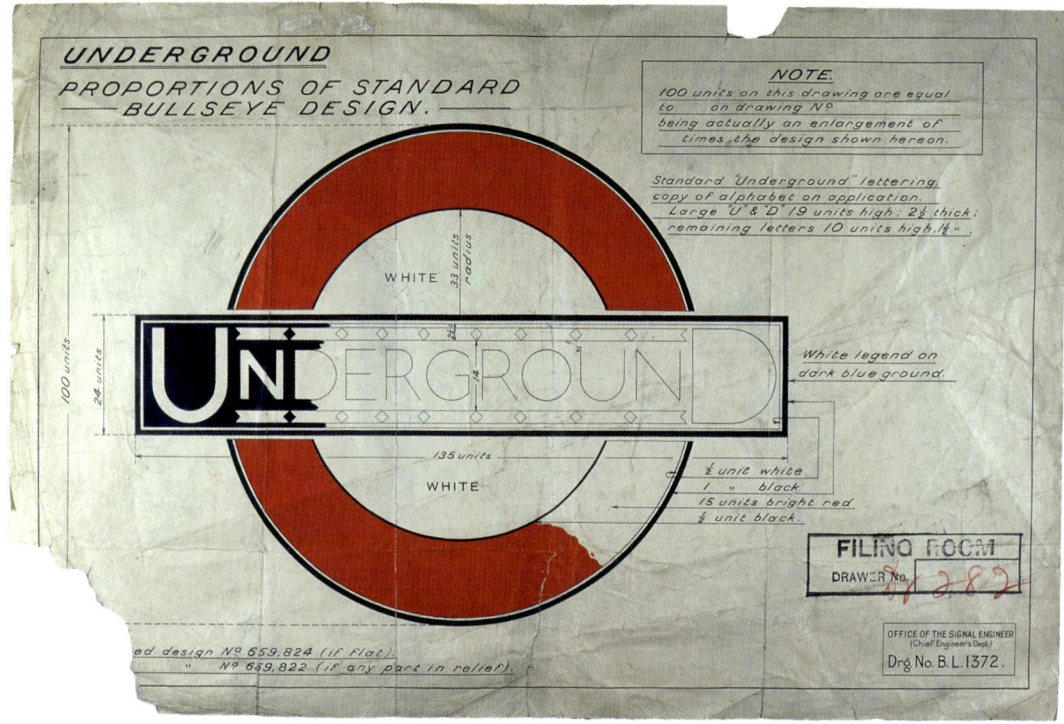

Above The earliest known surviving UERL design drawing (c.1925) showing Johnston's standard Underground bullseye. It was from the beginning, and still is, a registered trademark.

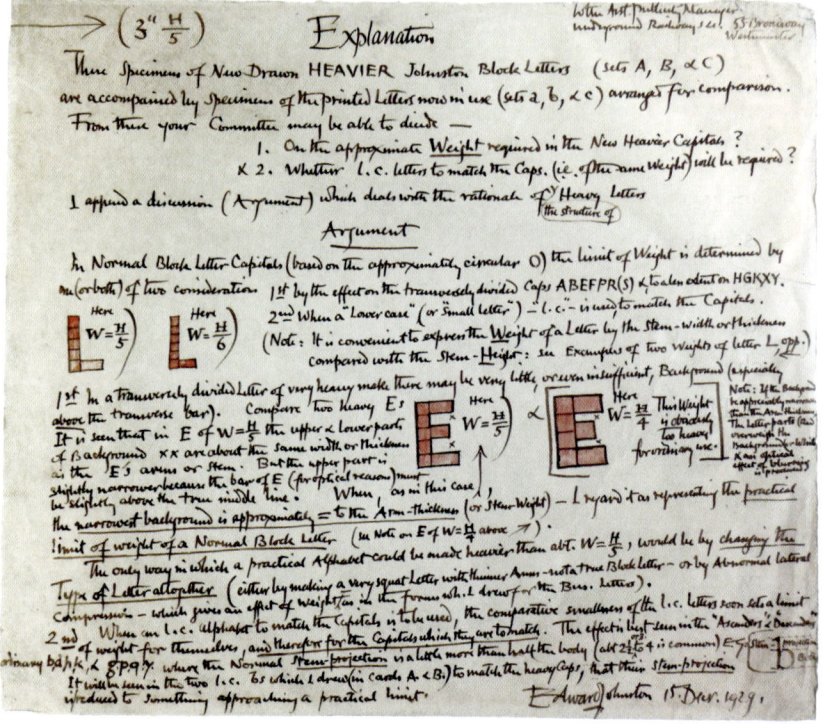

Right Extract from Johnston's letter to the UERL, 1929, accompanying his trial designs for the Johnston Bold letterform. In it Johnston explains the detailed calculations he used in amending the proportions of his original block letters to maintain legibility when used in the new bold face.

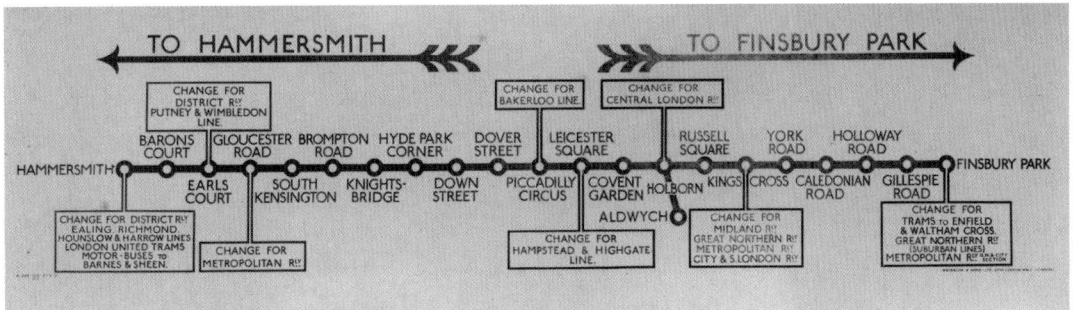

A 1916 line diagram for use inside carriages covering the original central section of the Piccadilly Railway (called the Piccadilly Line after 1933), using hand-drawn lettering based on the early Johnston capitals.

a few beautiful but costly objects as to give comeliness to the fashioning and decoration of the common things which we see and use daily.' [13] Whilst Johnston may have had reservations about what he referred to as 'Industrialism', his practical mind admitted that 'if you *will* travel in buses & tubes my block letters help to guide the passenger'; he even imagined his students saying, 'London is made a town fit for us to live in by Mr Johnston's letters.' [14]

Of course, Johnston's Underground lettering and logotype were by no means typical of his work. He certainly didn't regard himself as a graphic designer, and described himself variously as a 'letter-craftsman' or 'only a letterist or "Scribe" '. On becoming a CBE in 1939, he wrote in a letter to the Prime Minister's office, that it was difficult to describe his work, 'but the least unsatisfactory term for it seems to be calligrapher.' Peter Holliday has characterised him as 'fundamentally ... an artist craftsman doing jobbing work', but points out that Johnston was 'equally a thinker, a writer and a teacher. He set out to formulate a philosophy of the lettering arts ... He pointed to historical exemplars ... but he was forward-looking rather than historicist. He wanted letters to meet the needs of the contemporary, even urban world.' [15]

The two most frequently published photographs of Johnston show him in 1902 as a serious-looking youngish man working with a quill pen at his writing desk in Lincoln's Inn (*see* page 12), and in 1938 as the grand old man of lettering at home in Ditchling,

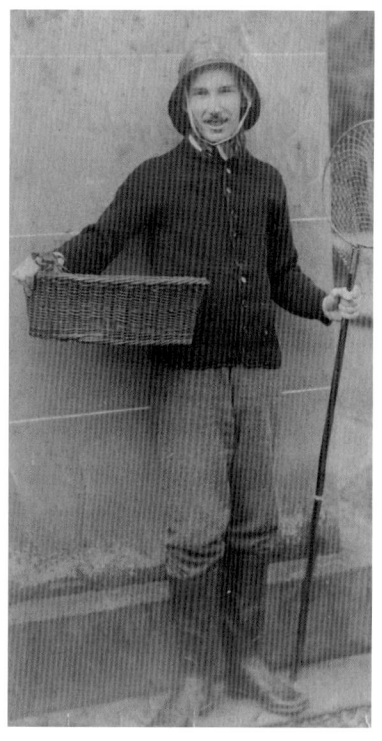
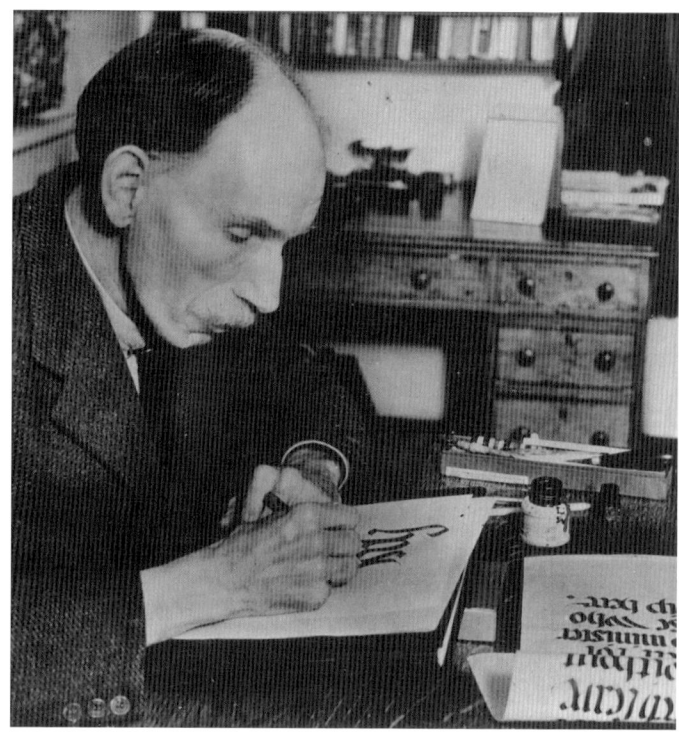

Above left Edward Johnston dressed as his ancestor 'Mussel Andrew', the son of a 17th-century Aberdeen fisherman; *right* Johnston in 1938, working on the inscription for the church porch at Kippen in Stirlingshire.

Sussex, still working on a manuscript. Viewing these slightly fusty images of the solitary craftsman at work a century on from the revolution in public lettering ushered in by Johnston, one could be forgiven for thinking of him as an austere and solitary Victorian, someone very distant from our own concerns. But this would be a mistake. Johnston's own writings, and the extensive collection of photographs still held by his family, reveal a man who revelled and thrived in the company of friends, family and colleagues: 'Self-taught and ever alert,' writes Peter Holliday, 'the stimulation of discourse was vital to him. Enquiry progressed through exacting discussion with like-minded friends and fellow-craftsmen ... Furthermore, these friendships often arose out of, or led to, creative collaborations ... He was drawn to such groups and, in turn, invariably became one of their focal points.' [16]

In *Writing & Illuminating & Lettering*, Johnston identifies 15th-century Italian formal writing as the source of the lower-case

> Omnes ſcti inocētes.   orate.
> Sancte Stephane.   ora.
> Sancte laurenti.   ora.
> Sancte vincenti.   ora.
> Sancte fabiane.   ora.
> Sancte ſebaſtiane.   ora.
> Sancte blaſi.   ora.
> Sācti Ioā. et paule   orate.
> Sācti Coſma et damia.   orate.

Detail of a page from a 16th-century Italian prayer book illustrated in Johnston's *Writing & Illuminating & Lettering*, 1906.

letters now standard in printed text. During the Renaissance, he relates, Italian scribes modelled their work on the 'beautiful Italian writing of the eleventh and twelfth centuries', and it was on these 'round clear letters' that early Italian printers then based their type. Thus, tradition, beauty and technology were combined to impressive effect. In the 21st century, Johnston's lively yet logical curiosity, combined with a joy in the humanity of his work, can still inspire. Ewan Clayton has highlighted the relevance to today's digital designers of Johnston's studies of the long manuscript tradition. Perhaps of even more significance is the potential for an understanding of calligraphy to assist inter-cultural communication, and especially in fostering a dialogue with the rich calligraphic traditions of the Islamic world. 'It is because Johnston took the link between his craft, his philosophy of life and its cultural roots so much to heart', writes Clayton, 'that Western calligraphers can engage so readily with their colleagues in the Middle East and Asia.' [17]

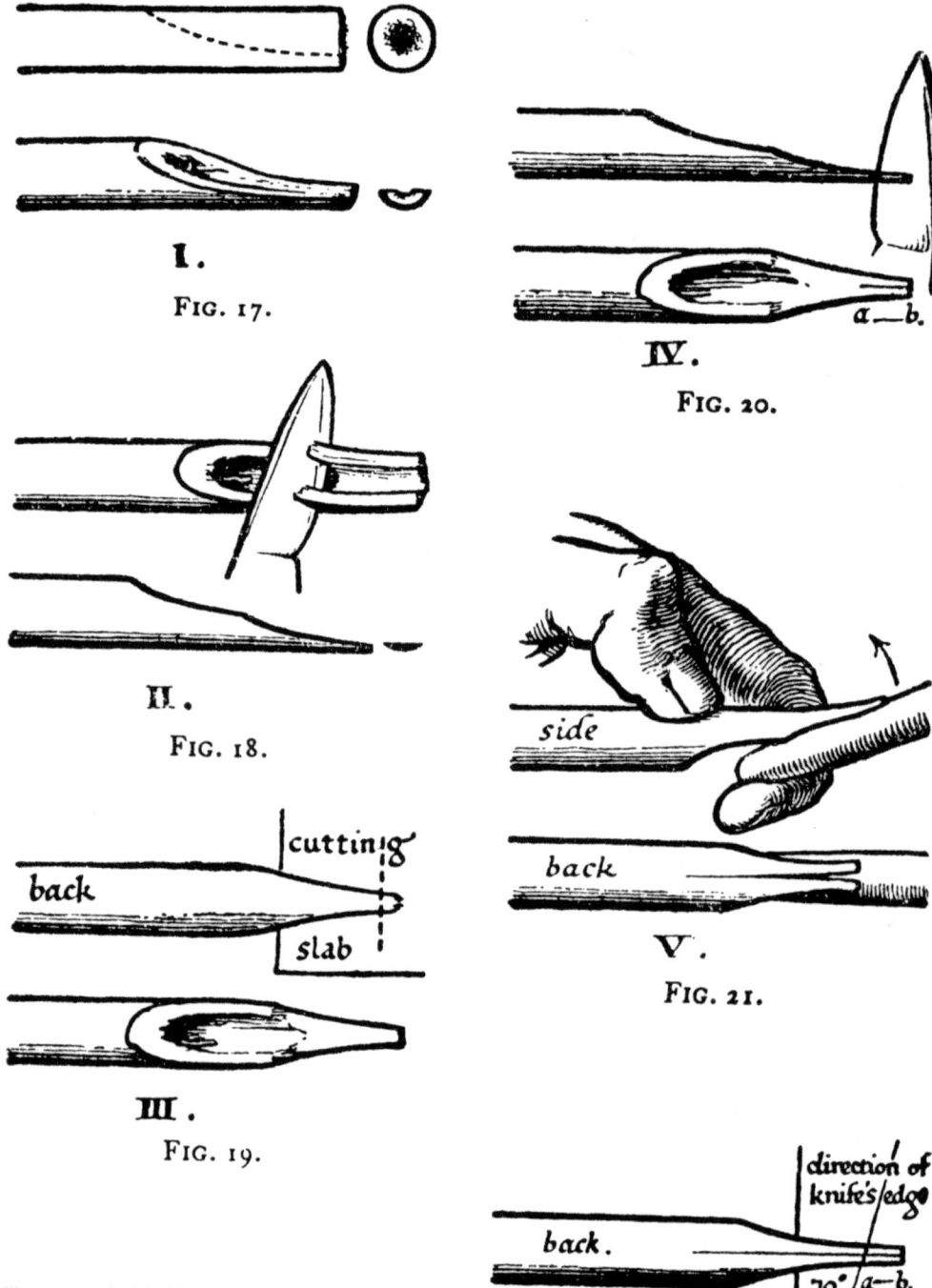

Illustrations by Noel Rooke from Johnston's *Writing & Illuminating & Lettering* (1906) demonstrating the importance that Johnston placed on correctly prepared, 'rightly handled' tools.

A CRAFTSMAN'S LIFE

This then is the scribe's direct purpose: the making of useful things legibly beautiful. Edward Johnston

Edward Johnston was born 'three-quarters Scotch' on 11th February 1872 at The Arazaty, his parents' remote ranch in the province of San José, Uruguay.[18] His paternal grandfather was the Scottish MP Andrew Johnston, of Rennyhill in Fife, who had married Priscilla Buxton, from Norfolk. The Buxtons were a prominent Quaker family who had been deeply involved in William Wilberforce's anti-slavery campaigns. They were related by marriage to two other elite Quaker merchant families, the Hanburys and the Gurneys, and through the latter to Elizabeth Fry (*née* Gurney), the early Victorian prison reform campaigner. After his marriage Andrew Johnston moved to Norfolk and joined the bank owned by his Gurney relatives (which later merged with that run by their cousins, the Barclays). His second son, Fowell Buxton Johnston (known as Buxton or Buck), was Edward Johnston's father.

The strong Quaker influence in Edward Johnston's extended family has been remarked upon by many, following Priscilla Johnston, as a key influence in the formation of Johnston's make-up and character. There is undoubtedly a certain amount of post-hoc reasoning in this view. Nonetheless it doesn't seem too much of a leap of faith to agree with Peter Holliday when he says of Johnston's later empathy with the ideals of the Arts and Crafts Movement: 'It was as though Johnston was naturally predisposed to that movement's distinctive ethos of simplicity in lifestyle, of straightforward usefulness in the making of things, and of a distaste for the contrived and the meretricious.' [19]

Several of the individuals who would be supportive of Johnston's development as an artist-craftsman had a Quaker or Non-conformist heritage, such as Frank Pick, Douglas Pepler, Eric Gill, and Gerard Tuke Meynell. 'Fitness for purpose must transcend the merely practical and serve a moral and spiritual order as well', wrote Frank Pick in 1933, his Congregationalist upbringing still evident in his attitude towards art and design. [20]

Buxton's elder brother, also called Andrew Johnston, was, it seems, the favoured sibling in both personality and achievement. In later life he was to become an MP, a JP, Clerk of Quarter Sessions, High Sheriff of Essex, Verderer of Epping Forest, and Chairman and so-called Father of Essex County Council. As Edward Johnston grew up it was to be 'Uncle Johnston' – Andrew – who discreetly guided and funded Edward's search for a vocation suited to his interests and temperament, culminating in supporting his nephew when he took his first steps as a professional calligrapher.

Buxton Johnston, by contrast, was characterised by Priscilla Johnston as 'an enigma, an erratically brilliant ne'er-do-well, contrary, original and highly eccentric … capricious and wilful.' [21] A series of fitful and unsuccessful attempts to establish a career was followed by the purchase of a commission in the 3rd Dragoon Guards, but while stationed in India with his regiment Buxton was struck down by a severe illness, and his military service was brought to an abrupt end. After his recovery he emigrated in 1866 to South America aged twenty-seven, apparently with a scheme in mind to make soap from wild horses; as with so much of his chaotic life the details of this enterprise remain obscure.

Three years after his arrival in Uruguay, Buxton married Alice Douglas, the daughter of another Scottish rancher. After her marriage, Alice brought her sister Maggie with her to The Arazaty where 'Aunty Maggie' became an inseparable part of the household and a major practical influence on Edward Johnston throughout his childhood. The family also included Miles Johnston, Edward's older brother, born in 1870, and two younger sisters – Ada, born 1874, and Olof, born 1883. (Priscilla Johnston relates the family story that when Olof was born, Buxton announced that she was to be called either Olof or Kettelred, or he would not come to the christening.) [22]

By the age of three, Edward Johnston had already crossed the Atlantic three times (on the first two occasions so that he could be christened in Scotland). The third time was a one-way trip in late 1874, or early 1875, when the ranch had been sold and the family was returning permanently to England, possibly because of Alice Johnston's physical fragility, or because Buxton's plans were not prospering. These two factors were to be ever-present throughout Edward Johnston's childhood.

Once back in England the Johnston family led what can only be described as a peripatetic and eccentric existence. They were constantly moving from place to place (although mainly in or near London) as Buxton, increasingly estranged from the family, pursued plans and opportunities, or because a new house was thought to be more suited to Alice's poor health. By the age of sixteen, Uruguayan-born Johnston had lived in Torquay, South Norwood, Hastings, Ventnor, Turnham Green, Upper Norwood, Balham, and Primrose Hill; in the next three years he was to move to Plymouth, Okehampton, Hampstead and Lewisham.

Probably due to her own frailty, Alice Johnston (who died in 1891 when Johnston was nineteen) seems to have lived in a state of constant anxiety about the health of her children, and her sister took this concern to extremes. Aunty Maggie seems to have been a classic hypochondriac, and it was she who effectively ran the domestic side of the household after the family's return to England. In Priscilla Johnston's retelling, she was obsessed with the dangers of draughts, colds and rain (and in summer with the heat and the dangers posed by thunderstorms), nursed a profound distrust of fresh air and open windows, and was insistent about the need to 'wrap up well' whatever the weather. Her fears seem to have been tragically borne out by the unexpected death in 1888 of Ada Johnston on her fourteenth birthday.

The combination of frequent domestic upheavals and enforced confinement – in some years being kept indoors, windows tight shut, from October until April – was probably the cause of Edward's lack of vigour and, later, an ingrained habit of passivity and slowness, characterised by Ewan Clayton as a 'learned response … almost … a coping mechanism' to deal with his circumscribed opportunities.[23]

These qualities were to become a two-edged sword for Edward in later years. On the one hand, they proved helpful in cultivating his patient craftsmanship and painstaking application to study; on the other they encouraged a tendency to procrastination and, when faced with work deadlines, to what we would now call displacement activity.

Priscilla Johnston tells resignedly of the inevitable routine that a calligraphy commission would follow when Edward was at the height of his fame. First came the 'Approach' from a client, either 'Municipal style' (brusque and businesslike) or 'Reverential' ('just write anything you like'). Then a pause, and then the letters would start. Initially optimistic ('it is now some months since we approached you'; 'I fear my last letter may have miscarried'), then anxiously asking for a 'reply by return'. Finally would come the urgent telegrams, followed by a burst of calligraphic activity and the last-minute dispatch of the manuscript by the most expeditious and often unconventional means. On one occasion Johnston is said to have finished a scroll only an hour before it was to be presented to the Prince of Wales some forty miles away, and he resorted to sitting beside the main road waiting for a motor car heading in the correct direction. After successfully hailing one and explaining the mission, the driver, 'being a loyal subject', delivered the document in the nick of time.[24]

None of the Johnston children received a conventional education; instead, they read on their own and were taught at home by their parents and a succession of tutors. Despite, or perhaps because of, this background, they all developed a lively intellectual curiosity. In addition to his mechanical and electrical experiments, and in an early foreshadowing of the direction he was to take in future, Edward made elaborate and humorous drawings for his sisters' amusement, and was absorbed by the popular Victorian hobby of 'illuminations' – rendering texts in the manner of a mediaeval manuscript. At the age of seventeen he was given a copy of W. J. Loftie's *Lessons in the Art of Illumination* (1880), one of many such popular hobbyist guides that spoke to the Victorian fascination with illuminated manuscripts. A significant omission from them all, though, was any information about the specific techniques used by mediaeval scribes, and it was these that Johnston was later to identify. In 1880, inspired by Loftie, Edward produced an ambitious 'parchment' for one of his aunts: a lush and heavily illuminated copy of the *Magnificat*. This revelation of talent provoked something of a sensation within the family, especially when a dealer acquaintance of Johnston's Uncle Andrew opined that the work was saleable. The dealer promptly commissioned a number of 'comic cards' which brought Edward his first earnings from his pen and almost certainly planted a seed in the mind of Andrew Johnston.

Following the death of Edward's mother Alice on 7th June 1891, Uncle Andrew, by then Chairman of Essex County Council, intervened to find Edward work in his office in New Broad Street, London EC4. It seems probable that Andrew also took on much of the care of the rest of the family, who were by that time living in New Cross. Buxton remained with them for a year after Alice Johnston's death, and then suddenly married again and departed, at which point the children and Aunty Maggie moved yet again, to Woodford in Essex, close to Andrew Johnston's house.

Johnston's post as office boy (he was later promoted to clerk) was intended by his uncle to provide some stability whilst Edward planned what to do with his adult life. This took some time, but by 1895 it had been decided (almost certainly for, not by, Edward) that he should become a doctor like his elder brother, including following in the footsteps of Miles to study medicine at Edinburgh University. Not having had a formal education, this required Edward to spend a year at the university's Preparatory Institute before starting his studies in autumn 1896. Initially Edward found the physics and chemistry interesting, but once his studies moved on to include the dissection of cadavers his interest turned to hatred. Andrew Johnston's family had been keeping an eye on him and became aware of his distress. Following medical consultations it was decided that Edward's constitution was not going to be up to the strains of a doctor's life, and it was agreed that he would leave the university at Easter in 1898. Edward's plans now consisted only of thoughts of returning to London and (the phrase is Gilbertian in its naivety) 'going in for Art'.

At this point there must have been some concern about Edward's future prospects. At twenty-six he was nearly the same age that Buxton had been when he emigrated to Uruguay and started on a long road of failing ever to make a steady living. The possibility of history repeating itself must have been at the back of his relatives' minds. And yet it was at exactly this point that the various strands of Edward's interests and personality finally, and successfully, came together.

The family plan was that, before resettling in London, Edward should go with his cousin Neil MacInnes on an adventurous summer

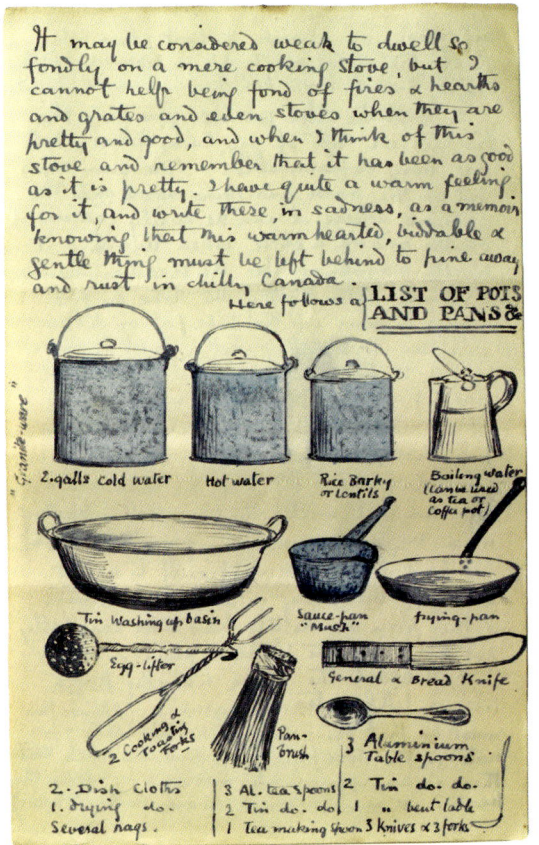
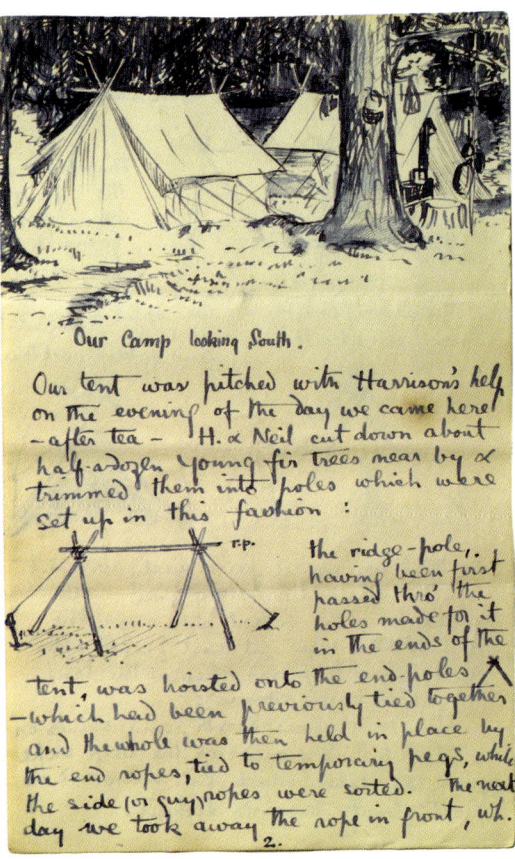

trip to Canada via the USA. (The trip eventually involved travelling to New York and then, via Chicago, to Salt Lake City, Seattle and onward for an extended stay camping on Salt Spring Island in British Columbia.) Priscilla Johnston explains that the plan came out of his relatives' concerns about his health. But it does not seem too much of an imaginative leap to suspect that Uncle Andrew may have seen the expedition as, at the very least, an opportunity to energise Edward, to shake him out of his drift and his habits of confinement. Certainly Edward's grandson (also, in the family tradition, named Andrew Johnston), who is now the custodian of Edward's photographs and diaries from this period, believes that Edward's encounter with 'the Wild West' did him nothing but good, allowing him physical and mental space to sharpen his thinking about what

Pages from Edward Johnston's diary for 1898 that describe pitching camp on Salt Spring Island, British Columbia, with his cousin Neil MacInnes and a companion called Harrison, and their cooking arrangements.

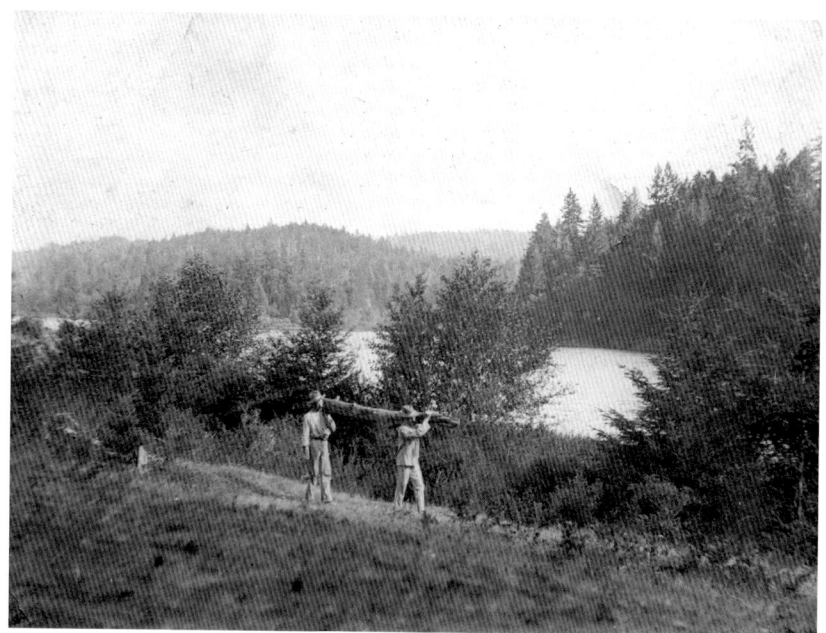

Edward Johnston and his cousin Neil MacInnes camping on Salt Spring Island, summer 1898. In the photograph taken inside their tent, Edward Johnston is on the left.

he wanted to do when he returned to England. And prior to his departure Edward had indeed been given plenty to think about.

Before embarking for New York Edward spent three weeks in London making his preparations. He later called the events of those weeks 'the miracle of my life'. Ewan Clayton has remarked that 'If this [trip to London] had not happened the whole development of calligraphy, typography and letter-cutting in Britain might well have followed a different path, and even some aspects of our modern tools of digital communication might have been different in their look and feel. Their current form is not so inevitable as it sometimes seems.' [25]

Edward stayed in London with the MacRaes, family friends originally from Scotland. The MacRaes knew the architect and amateur illuminator William Harrison (Harry) Cowlishaw, who was later to collaborate with Charles Holden, architect of the Underground railway extensions constructed in the 1920s and 1930s.[26] Johnston was already an admirer of Cowlishaw's

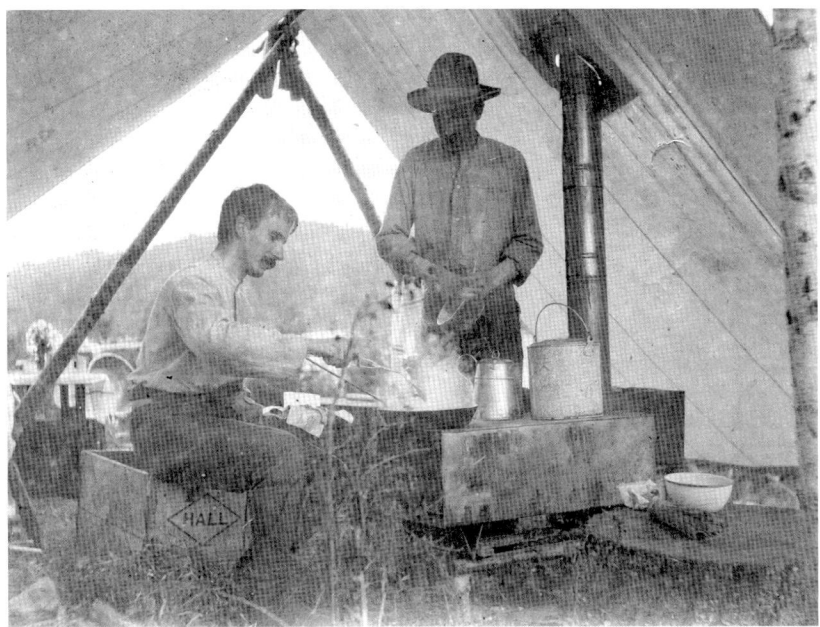

illuminations in *The Artist* magazine, and Mollie MacRae had shown Cowlishaw some samples of Johnston's own parchments, whose encouraging remarks were then reported by Mollie to Johnston.

On the morning of Johnston's arrival in London – 4th April 1898 – Cowlishaw paid a visit to the MacRaes. Johnston asked him for advice about 'going in for Art' as a way of making a living; Cowlishaw's response was to take Johnston straight round to Gray's Inn Road to meet his friend William Lethaby. Looking back in later years, Johnston often remarked on this as having been nothing less than 'a Divine providence': on his first day in London he had been taken to the person described by Priscilla Johnston as 'the one, the *only* man who could have helped him'.

Lethaby was also an architect. A former clerk to Norman Shaw, he was an early member of the Society for the Protection of Ancient Buildings, and had been a friend of William Morris. In 1894 he had started working for the Technical Education Board of the newly formed London County Council and in 1896 he had founded the Central School of Arts and Crafts. The Central School was dedicated to breaking down the barriers between the academic study of design and the development and promotion of craftsmanship skills. 'Only daily-work art is worth a button,' Lethaby said, 'all the High variety is disease. All that art-teaching is like learning to swim in a thousand lessons without water.'

Lethaby urged Johnston to set aside his vaguely expressed ideas of 'learning to draw' in favour of taking up a practical craft skill from which a living could always be earned, such as silversmithing or bookbinding. This latter example may well have prompted Johnston to mention his parchments; in any case the conversation so inspired Johnston that he visited Lethaby again the next day to show him examples of his calligraphy. Like Cowlishaw, Lethaby saw potential in Johnston's work. He praised the manuscripts warmly, expressed his confidence that this indeed could be Johnston's *métier*, and urged Edward to develop his knowledge and skills by studying mediaeval manuscripts in the British Museum Library. To this end Lethaby was later to introduce Johnston to Sydney Cockerell, William Morris's former secretary, and a manuscript collector and scholar, who would act as a supervisor for Johnston's research.[27]

More practically, Lethaby immediately commissioned a piece of decorative writing from Johnston. This may well have been intended as a test, because on its prompt delivery eleven days later Lethaby not only paid Johnston thirty shillings for the work, but also offered him from the following autumn a post teaching at his proposed new 'illuminating class' at the Central School. Johnston's mind must have been in a whirl on his voyage across the Atlantic.

For various administrative reasons the new class did not in fact start until the autumn of 1899. This delay allowed Edward a full year to immerse himself in the careful study of manuscripts and, in Ewan Clayton's words, to realise that 'his interests were grounded

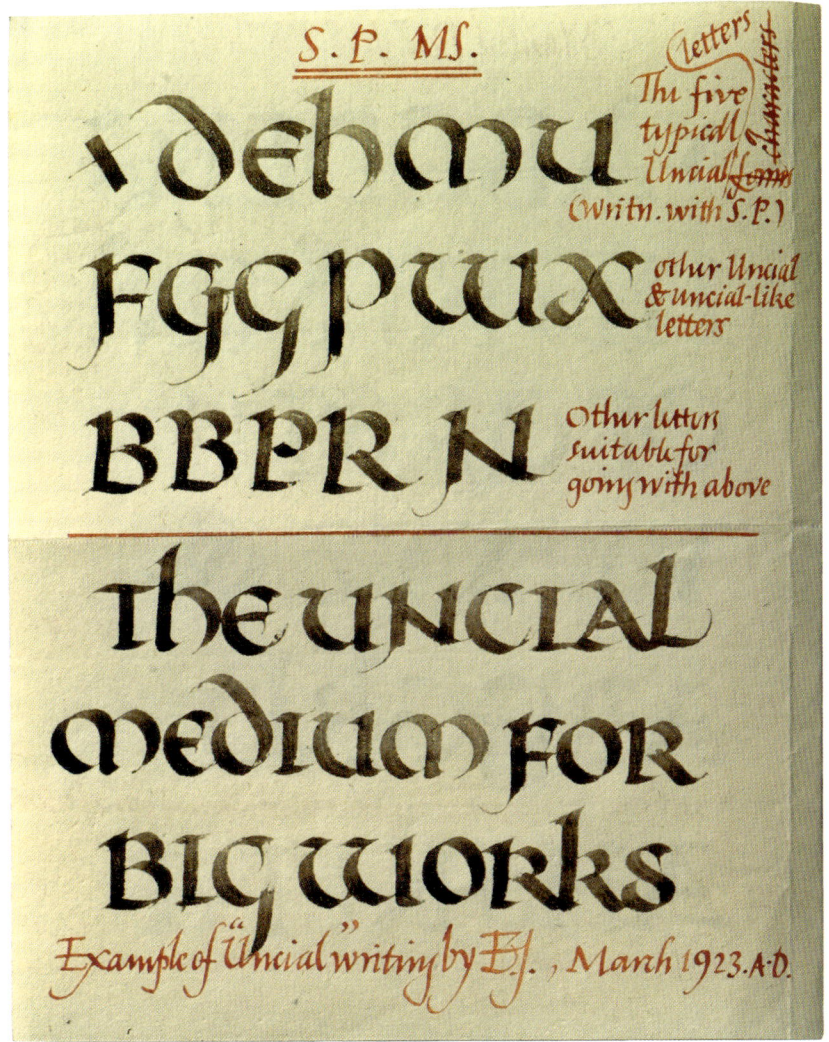

Roman Uncial lettering drawn in pen and ink on paper by Johnston in 1923 when he was teaching at the Royal College of Art, London.

in a tradition with a long, and by then almost-forgotten, history of producing legible, expedient and serviceable letter-forms.'[28] It was Cockerell who guided Johnston to an understanding of how Italian Renaissance scribes had re-established Roman capitals and the Carolingian-based forms that we know today as lower-case letters. His realization that the scribes had in turn influenced the work of medieval printers persuaded Johnston that, rather than simply giving classes on Victorian 'illuminating', his teaching should rework and re-establish the tradition of hand-lettering.[29]

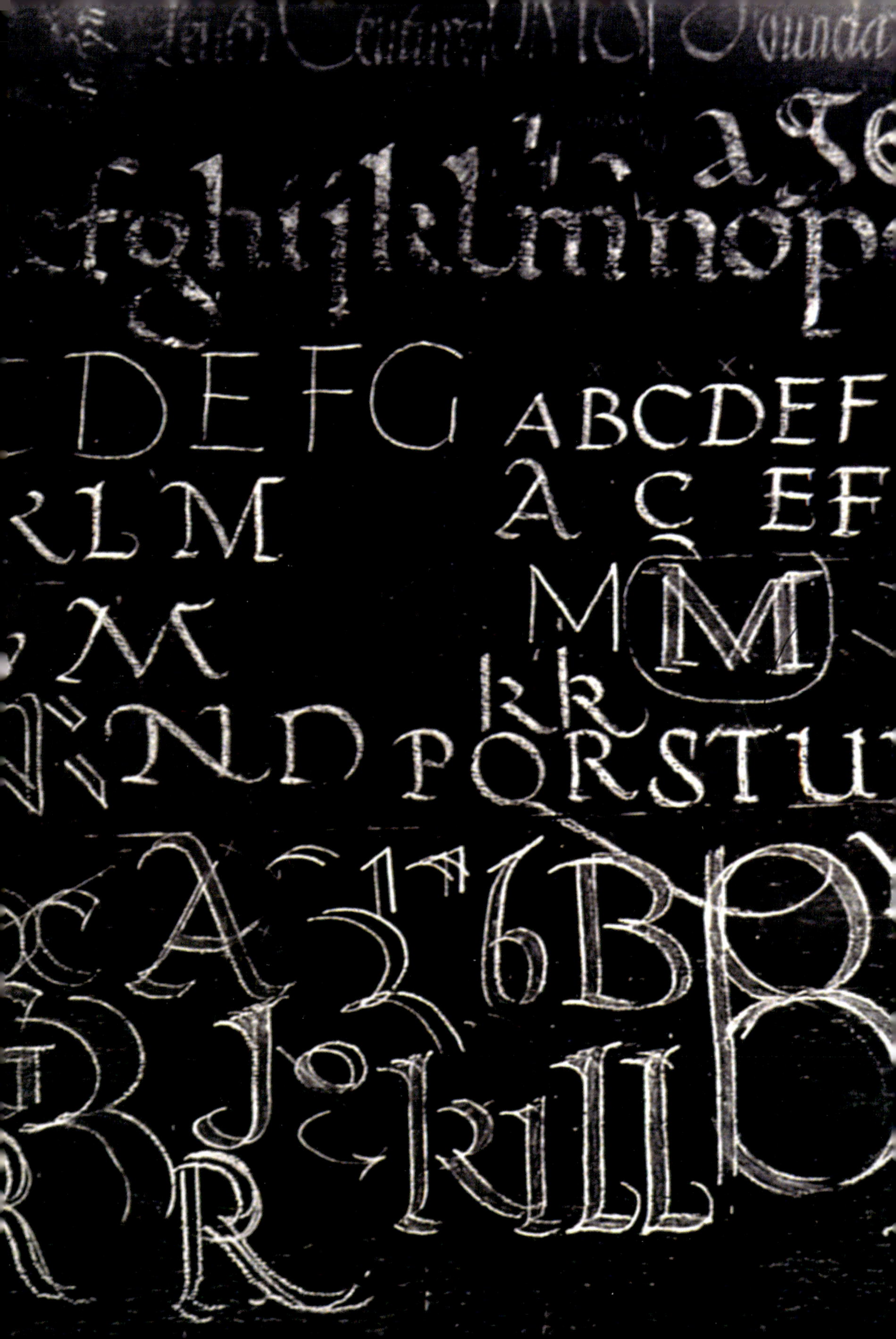

efghijklmnop

DEFG ABCDEF
LM   A C EF
M   MM
ND   kk
     PORSTU

A 16 B
J
R RKLL

Johnston taught his first class, of seven students, on 21st September 1899. This was the start of over thirty years of teaching in the course of which Johnston created and influenced a generation of artist/craft workers. Those attending his classes during that first year included Noel Rooke, Graily Hewitt, T. J. Cobden-Sanderson, Percy Smith, Eric Gill and his brother Leslie MacDonald Gill.[30]

Eric Gill later recalled 'the thrill and the tremble of the heart' that he experienced the first time he saw Johnston write; he was to become the most famous disciple of the Johnstonian approach to lettering. When the Monotype Corporation released his Gill Sans typeface in 1928 Gill wrote to Johnston to say that he was taking 'every opportunity of proclaiming the fact that what [Monotype] call *"Gill" sans* owes all its goodness to your Underground letter.'[31]

Johnston was an effective teacher who inspired affection and devotion in his students. He was not afraid to criticise students' work but was also confident enough to bring humour into the classroom; he had, for example, a fondness for quoting from *Alice in Wonderland*. Thanks to the foresight of one of his students, Violet Hawkes, photographs were taken of his classroom blackboards (now in the collections of Central St Martins College and the Crafts Study Centre), allowing his pedagogical method to be analysed. Although this dynamic and engaging teacher may sound very unlike the old Johnston, his painstaking style remained evident. Edward Bawden later recalled attending a Johnston class at the Royal College of Art in 1920. After a solid hour having the characteristics of the letter 'A' demonstrated on a blackboard, Bawden concluded that the chances of ever reaching 'Z' were so remote that he never attended another of Johnston's classes.[32]

In stark contrast to the previous somewhat directionless decade, Johnston was now busier with each year that passed. In 1901, Lethaby was appointed as the first Professor of Design at the Royal College of Art. Soon after he invited Johnston to start a

Detail from a photograph of the blackboard used by Johnston in his lectures at the Royal College of Art, London, in 1926.

STAND STILL, true poet that you are,   **POPULAR-**
    I know you; let me try and draw you.   **ITY**
Some night you'll fail us. When afar
    You rise, remember one man saw you,
Knew you, and named a star.

My star, God's glow-worm! Why extend
    That loving hand of His which leads you,
Yet locks you safe from end to end
    Of this dark world, unless He needs you—
Just saves your light to spend?

His clenched Hand shall unclose at last
    I know, and let out all the beauty.
My poet holds the future fast,
    Accepts the coming ages' duty,
Their present for this past.

That day, the earth's feast-master's brow
    Shall clear, to God the chalice raising;
"Others give best at first, but Thou
    For ever set'st our table praising,—
Keep'st the good wine till now."

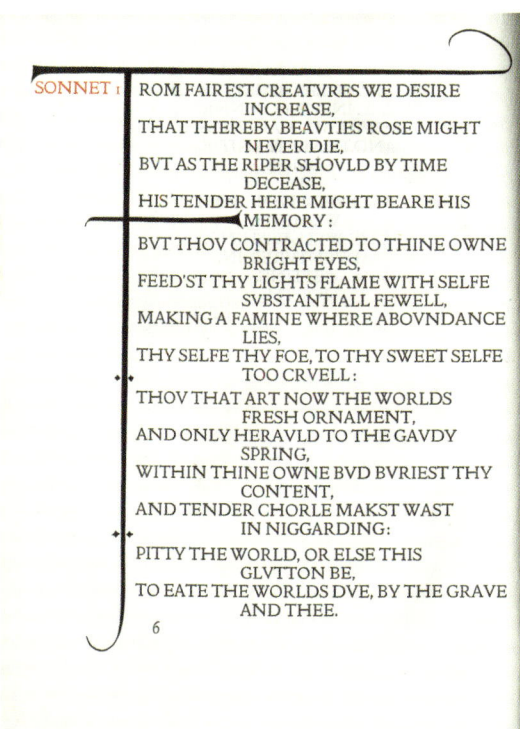

class there, which Johnston was to maintain for over twenty-five years (he ceased to lecture at the Central School in 1912). At the same time T. J. Cobden-Sanderson was making plans to start his private Doves Press in partnership with Emery Walker, who had been William Morris's typographical advisor. Cobden-Sanderson had dreams of setting up an associated scriptorium where Johnston could create work for this new venture, and as a start he commissioned Johnston to write out on vellum the text of Cobden-Sanderson's manifesto *The Ideal Book or Book Beautiful*, printed and published by Doves Press in 1900. In the spring of 1902, the first mentions appear in Johnston's correspondence of his own manifesto which was to become *Writing & Illuminating & Lettering*. In this book, published in 1906, Johnston set out his creed that lettering should always aspire to the qualities of 'Readableness, Beauty and Character'.

Two pages from the tercentenary edition of *Shakespeare's Sonnets* published by the Doves Press in 1909, with three initial capitals designed by Edward Johnston and engraved by Noel Rooke and Eric Gill. 250 copies were printed on paper, fifteen on vellum.

Opposite Page from the 1908 Doves Press edition of Robert Browning's *Men & Women* (1855), with flourishes in red, blue and green ink by Edward Johnston. Thirteen copies, like this one, were printed on vellum, hence its translucence.

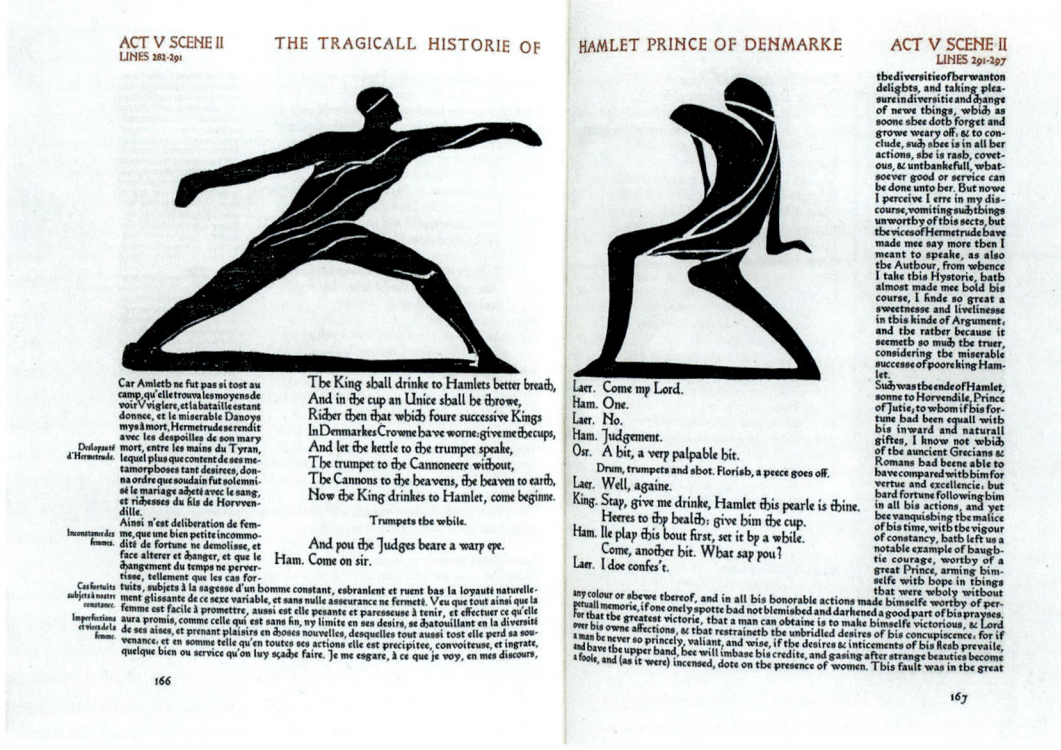

Pages taken from one of the best-known publications of the Cranach Press: *The Tragedie of Hamlet Prince of Denmark* (1930), with illustrations by Edward Gordon Craig. Kessler commissioned Johnston to create a typeface to be used throughout the book. The resulting Cranach Press Italic was inspired by the work of a Venetian scribe.

The *Book Beautiful* commission led not only to further orders for Johnston but also fired his interest in letterforms for printing. Between 1911 and 1914 Johnston was asked by the anglophile German publisher Count Harry Kessler to design italic, blackletter and Greek typefaces for Kessler's private Cranach Press in Weimar. This interest in type design was soon to lead Johnston into the orbit of the printer and publisher Gerard Tuke Meynell, owner of the Westminster Press.

In 1912 Meynell had decided to launch *The Imprint*, a short-lived journal campaigning for higher standards in printing and typography. One of Meynell's partners was J. H. Mason, Cobden-Sanderson's former compositor at Doves Press and a former pupil of Johnston. Mason invited Johnston to join them as lettering editor. The masthead of The Imprint was reproduced from Johnston's calligraphy, and a very young Stanley Morison

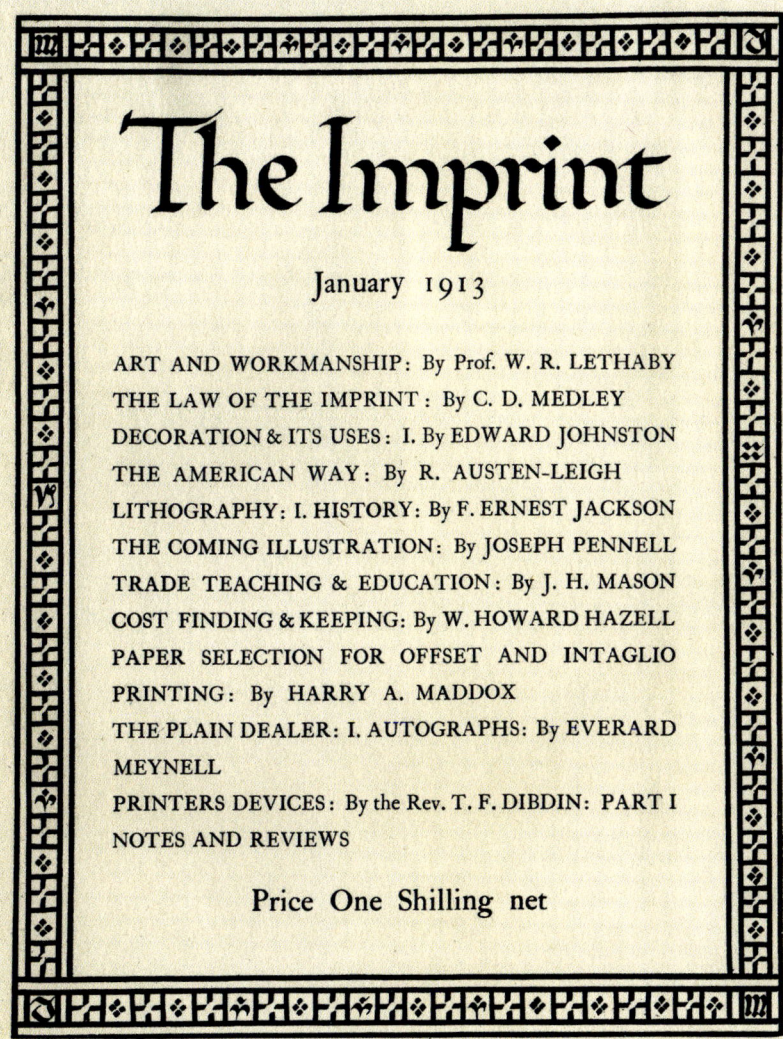

The first issue of *The Imprint*, which ran to nine issues from January to November 1913. Edward Johnston, one of the founders and editors, designed the masthead and border ornament shown here as well as contributing articles to the magazine.

joined the staff as an office boy. One of the Westminster Press's clients was the Underground Electric Railways Group of London (UERL), and it was Meynell who, on 16th June 1913, introduced Johnston to Frank Pick, Commercial Manager of the Group. This meeting ultimately resulting in the commissioning of Johnston's Standard Block Lettering for the Underground and the London Underground 'bullseye' symbol, to the story of which we will return.

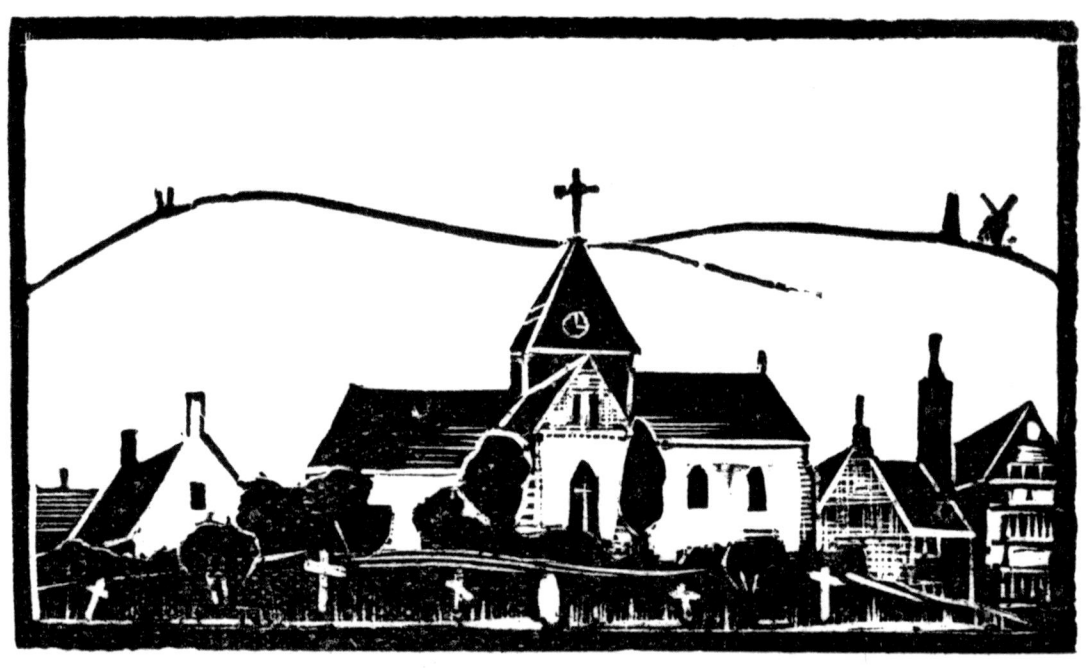

Wood-cut views of Ditchling, from the *Guide Book of Ditchling*, 1926, published at Sun Down Tea Room and Garden and printed by Douglas Pepler at the St Dominic's Press, Ditchling.

During this period Johnston's private and domestic life was also transformed. In 1901 he moved into a tiny flat in Lincoln's Inn, shared with his pupil Eric Gill and a small cat (it was here that the well-known photographs of a serious young Johnston at his writing table were taken – *see* page 12). But this bachelor existence was shortlived. The year before, on a weekend visit to his MacInnes cousins in North Berwick, Johnston had met a friend of Dora MacInness called Greta Grieg, an Oxford history graduate working as a schoolteacher near London. The two seem to have made an immediate impression on each other, such that when they met again in London the following May they were engaged within a month: a 'lightning courtship so astonishingly uncharacteristic of the slow and cautious Mr Johnston'.[33]

Greta and Edward Johnston married in August 1903 and initially moved to 4 Gray's Inn, next-door to Lethaby's offices. With the imminent arrival of their first daughter the Johnstons moved again to 3 Hammersmith Terrace in West London, the house which

A CRAFTSMAN'S LIFE

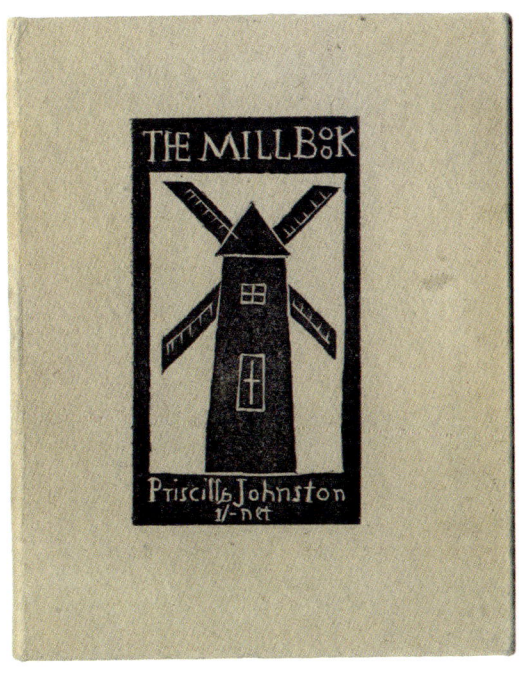 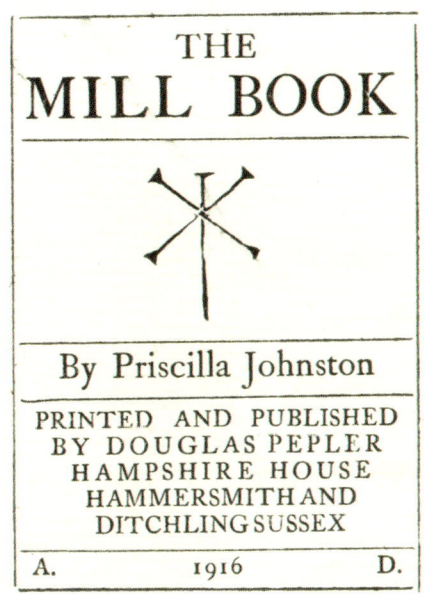

Cover and title page of *The Mill Book* (1916) inspired by a visit to a village mill by Johnston's five-year-old daughter Priscilla who wrote a story about it as a birthday present for her mother. She drew the pictures herself and dictated the words to her father. Douglas Pepler took a fancy to the story and published it using woodcuts based on Priscilla's drawings made by his son David and another boy.

now bears Johnston's blue plaque. In 1905 the district was a hotbed of the Arts and Crafts Movement. Local residents included Emery Walker (who was also Johnston's landlord), T. J. Cobden-Sanderson, and Eric Gill and his family. Soon to move into the area was Douglas Pepler, a pioneer social worker, member of the Fabian Society and Quaker.[34] This community was closely entwined socially and professionally: for example, Pepler, though he was already experimenting with craft printing, actually first met and got to know Johnston through their children's friendship.

Soon, though, Eric Gill was able to fulfil his ideal of living as a self-sufficient rural craftsman and in 1907 moved his growing family to the secluded village of Ditchling in Sussex. It was perhaps inevitable that others would follow, and in 1912 the Johnstons moved there, to be joined in 1914 by the Peplers. Despite Miles Johnston's concerns that the move would cut his brother off from sources of work in London, the relocation benefited the health of both Greta and Edward Johnston, and they lived in Ditchling for the rest of their lives.

The following years – 1912 to 1920 – were the most productive of Johnston's career. The Johnston, Gill and Pepler triumvirate became the nucleus of an extensive community of artists and craftsmen centred on the village. The three friends were inseparable. They argued about their work until late into the night, taught each other Latin, produced a magazine (*The Game*) expressing their ideals, and scoured the countryside for a suitable dwelling which could be converted to provide a home for their vision of a craft-guild founded on communal living and prayer. In 1916 these plans moved towards reality when the Johnstons and the Peplers jointly purchased Halletts Farm, close to the Gills' home on the edge of Ditchling Common.

Unfortunately, rather than heralding a new beginning the move to Halletts instead marked a highpoint in Johnston's association with Gill and Pepler that was never to be reached again. 'As so often happens,' writes Priscilla Johnston, 'the whole venture had been more buoyantly enthralling in anticipation than it proved in fact'; religious differences between the friends become more apparent and eventually caused them to drift apart. [35]

Gill had converted to Roman Catholicism in 1913, and Pepler followed suit in 1917, but the resolutely Anglican Johnston refused to do likewise. As Priscilla Johnston relates, 'To Gill and Pepler it seemed wrong of course that their little brotherhood of three should be divided on so important an issue. Here now was a matter for midnight arguments of such urgency and moment as to overshadow all else.' [36] Nonetheless, Johnston, stiffened by Greta's strong opposition, firmly excluded himself from Gill's and Pepler's plans, and the friends' regular contact fell away. Gill and Pepler took over production of *The Game,* turning it into the official voice of what was to become the (craft) Guild of St Joseph and St Dominic. The Guild was based at Halletts where the Johnstons also continued to live, rather awkwardly one imagines, until they moved back to Ditchling village in 1920. Four years later,

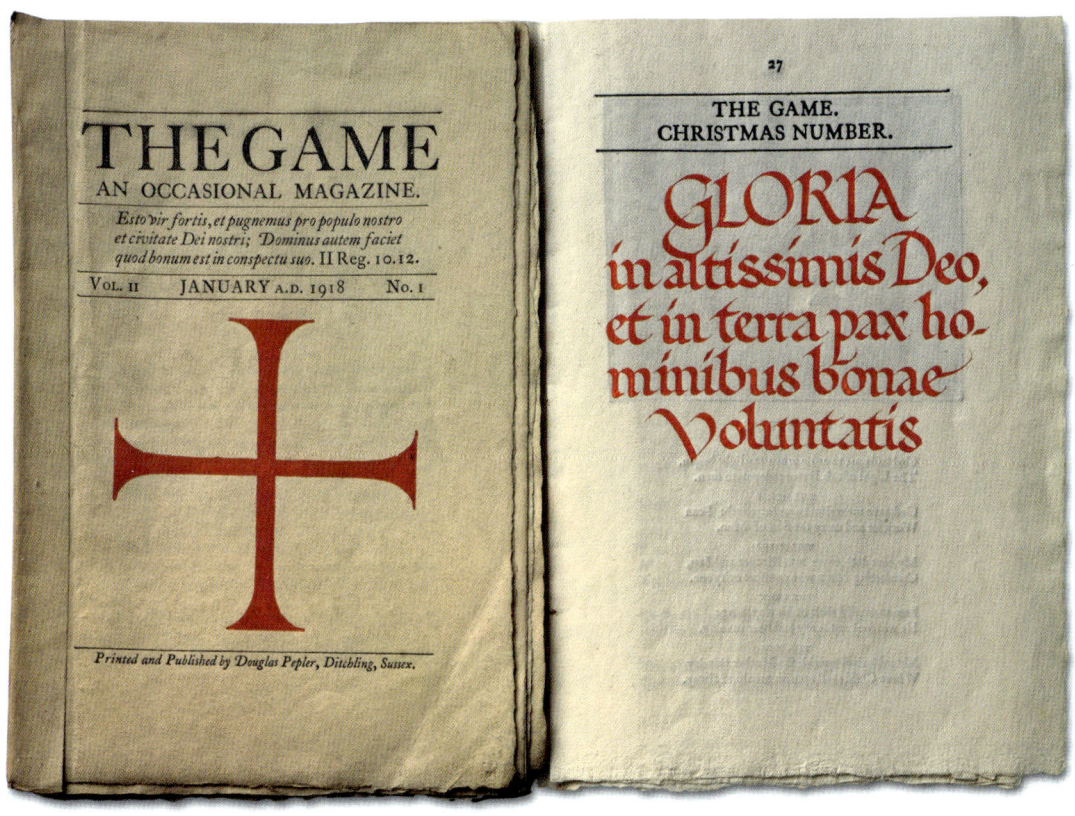

Cover and page from Vol. 2 No. 1 and Vol. 1 No. 2 of *The Game*, a magazine published between 1916 and 1922 by Douglas Pepler and edited (and mainly written) by Pepler, Eric Gill and Edward Johnston. The type and original calligraphy are in black and vermilion ink. Johnston wrote an inscription into each copy of the Christmas 1916 issue.

Gill's and Pepler's partnership itself fell apart, and Gill moved to Wales. Ewan Clayton has speculated that, without the grounding influence of Johnston, the dynamic between Gill and Pepler proved to be inherently unstable.[37]

After Gill's departure, Johnston's life in Ditchling gradually became more reclusive, and his days were spent largely on work and thought, punctuated until 1927 by his weekly London trips to lecture at the Royal College of Art and his continued work as a consultant for Frank Pick at the Underground Group (from 1933, the London Passenger Transport Board). In 1934 Johnston became President of the Arts and Crafts Exhibition Society, a post from which he resigned after the death of his wife in 1936. He returned to the Royal College in 1938, after a long break, to give a final series of three lectures, but by this time his eyesight was beginning to fail and he had ceased to undertake commissions.

In 1939 Johnston was awarded the CBE. In 1940 he executed his very last commissioned manuscript, an inscription made as a retirement gift for Frank Pick (*see* page 67). That same year Eric Gill died, followed by Frank Pick in 1941. In 1943 Johnston suffered a serious bout of pneumonia from which he probably never fully recovered, and he died, aged 72, on 26th November 1944. He is buried in Ditchling churchyard with his wife, close to where Douglas Pepler would also be buried in 1951. Appropriately, the inscription on Edward and Greta Johnston's headstone was carved by Joseph Cribb, Eric Gill's first apprentice. The Ditchling Museum of Art and Craft, a fitting memorial to the community the Johnstons helped to found, now stands next to the churchyard.

Hand-painted destination plates for tube trains on the Northern City and extended Northern Lines, post 1935. Handwork, in principle so close to Johnston's own working ethos, inevitably introduces variations, as close inspection of these plates shows. The line never, in fact, ran as far as Bushey Heath as this final extension fell victim to post-war austerity; the planned depot site was eventually used for Aldenham Bus Overhaul Works.

DRAYTON PK

BUSHEY HEATH

MORDEN

East FINCHLEY

TOOTING

HIGH BARNET

FINCHLEY CEN

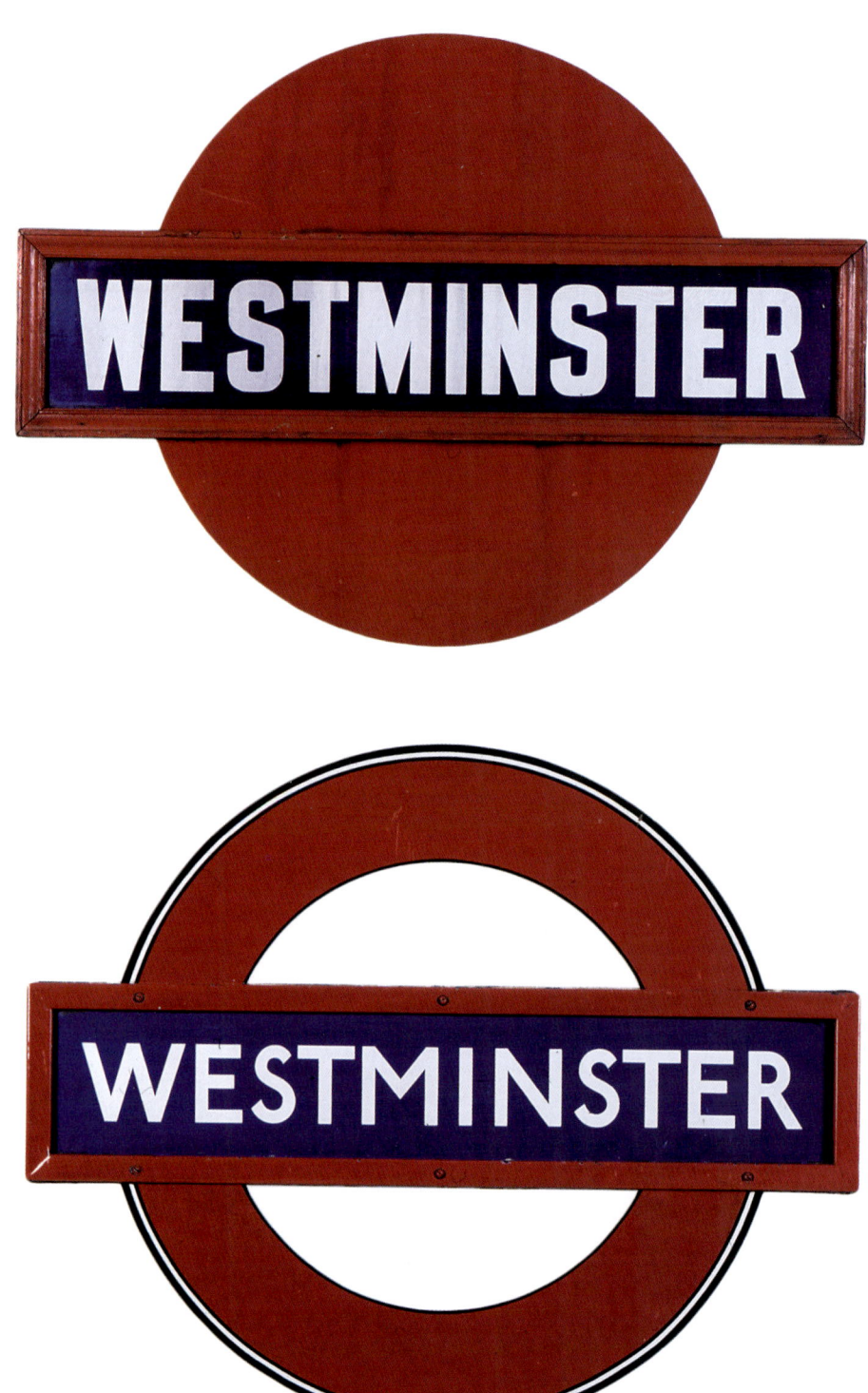

JOHNSTON AND LONDON

The letters at Railway Stations, street corners & other places, enamelled in white on blue are quite striking (when you know where to look for them) but they would be better if the blue ground were made a little larger & darker & of course the forms of the letters might be improved ... Much might be done in arrangement of neighbouring signs, & in having stated places for important signs, as at stations, so that we would know where to look for them. It is no good each trying to shout louder than his neighbour: that way madness or deafness lies. Edward Johnston, 1906 [38]

Johnston shared with Douglas Pepler and Eric Gill an affection for many of the indigenous British sans-serif letterforms such as 'grotesques' and 'fat faces' which had evolved in the 19th century, and by 1906 he had become interested in public lettering. Justin Howes recounts Noel Rooke's story of how he, Johnston and Gill emerged from the Central School in 1906 to see a railway van with really good block lettering on its tarpaulin, to which Gill had remarked 'I wish I could do that!' [39]

By this time Johnston had also met and produced some inscriptions for Count Harry Kessler which would lead to further typographical commissions; as a result of Kessler's patronage, Johnston gained a high reputation in Germany (*see* page 36). Ironically, in the early years of the 20th century, a number of British industrialists began to express concern about competition from better-designed and marketed German goods, and in 1915 the Design and Industries Association (DIA) was set up,

Opposite, above: the original solid red disc used in station signage before Johnston's bullseye. This is the Metropolitan District Railway variant from 1911, using a slightly smaller disc than on the deep-level tubes. The condensed lettering is a late 19th century sans-serif typeface, identified by Mark Ovenden as a variant on Franklin Gothic; below: its replacement, a standard Johnston bullseye dating from 1924. In both cases the red wooden frame around the station name is not structural but simply glued on.

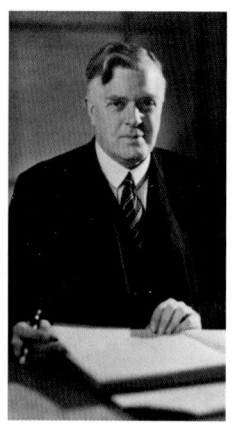

Frank Pick, 1939.

modelled on the Deutscher Werkbund (the German Association of Craftsmen) founded in 1907 to bring manufacturers and craftsmen together at the instigation of Herman Muthesius, author of a three-volume survey of the British Arts and Crafts Movement.[40] One of the founder members of the DIA was Frank Pick of Underground Electric Railways of London.

Pick (1878-1941) was born in Lincolnshire and educated in York. There he started his career as a solicitor, before joining the North Eastern Railway headquarters staff in York in 1902; he soon became assistant to the General Manager, George Gibb. Gibb was a pioneer in adopting American management techniques and in 1906 he was head-hunted by UERL to become their Managing Director (the company was heavily backed by American investors), whereupon Gibb invited Pick to follow him south.

At that time UERL controlled the long-established Metropolitan District Railway, and three new deep-level 'tube' railways opened in 1906 (the Charing Cross, Euston and Hampstead Railway; the Baker Street and Waterloo Railway; and the Great Northern, Piccadilly and Brompton Railway). The group was soon faced with financial crisis: the result of having to meet hefty interest payments on the tube lines' construction costs and generating lower fare income than had been anticipated.

To help tackle the problem Gibb recruited, in 1908, a new General Manager for UERL called Albert Stanley. Stanley (later Lord Ashfield) was a hard-headed American tramway manager of British origin. Perhaps to the surprise of some, the aesthetically minded Pick, whose background was austere and Congregationalist, quickly formed an effective managerial partnership with the ruthless and worldly Stanley. With Pick focusing on publicity and commercial matters, and Stanley on politics and financial management, their partnership would eventually, in 1933, result in the creation of the unified London Passenger Transport Board, soon to be known

Opposite A selection of signs that are both precursors and imitators of the UERL bullseye, all dating from before 1933.

JOHNSTON AND LONDON

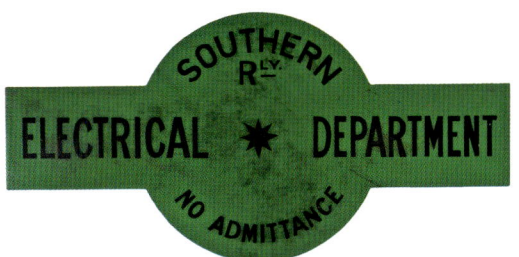

Left Southern Railways enamel sign (1930) inspired by the UERL roundel.

Right The London General Omnibus Company (LGOC) winged wheel and crossbar badge, introduced from 1905. LGOC was acquired by UERL in 1912.

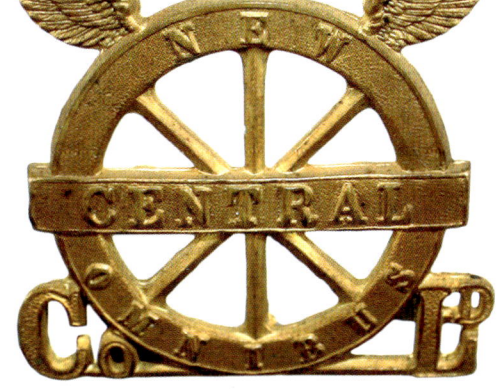

Right A First World War YMCA Hut Day pin showing the bar and hollow triangle that, at Frank Pick's suggestion, inspired Johnston's bullseye.

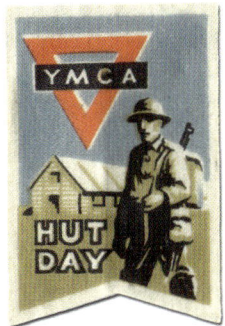

Right Green diamond station nameboard (pre-dating the Metropolitan red diamond) from Shoreditch on the East London Railway, designed and installed in 1912-13 (following electrification of the ELR) by the District Engineer's Office, against Frank Pick's wishes.

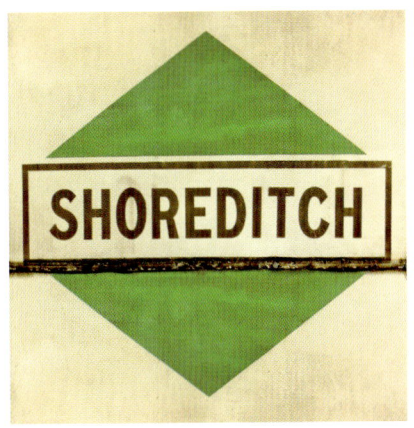

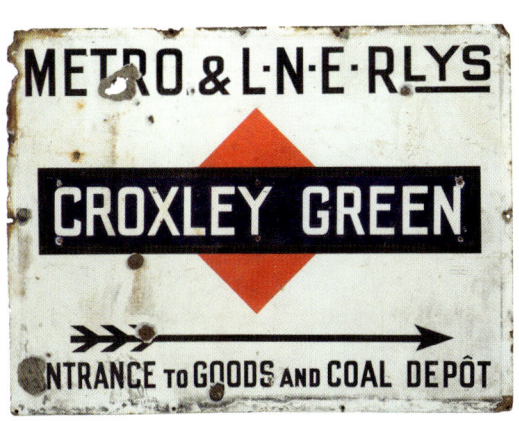

Left Metropolitan & London North Eastern Railway metal sign (1923-33): the red diamond and bar logo which came into use from around 1913. Clearly inspired by the UERL solid disc, all such signs were quickly removed following the Met's incorporation into the UERL-dominated London Transport (1933).

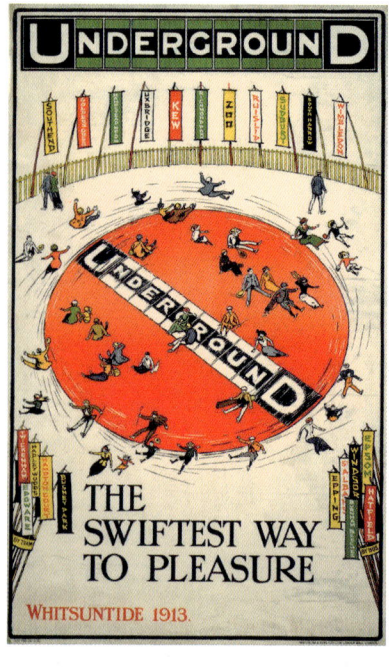
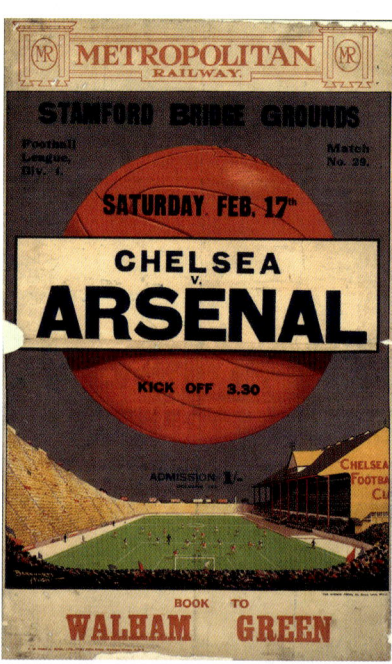

Before Johnston's designs, the proportions of the disc in the UNDERGROUND logo were not fixed, as seen here in a poster by Charles Sharland, 1913 (left) and the cheeky pastiche for the Metropolitan Railway of the UERL disc and bar logo by Bernhard Hugh, 1923 (right).

Opposite Monument Station entrance in 1916, an example of the interim style of branding after the introduction of the UNDERGROUND wordmark but still using 19th-century block lettering.

Early in 1908 a joint committee of transport operators was persuaded by Albert Stanley to adopt the word 'Underground' as their collective branding. Soon after, the word was given enlarged initial and terminal letters; sometimes it was combined with a stylised silhouette of the London skyline, as seen here in John Hassall's poster of 1908 (the logo was added to Hassall's original artwork). The silhouette branding fell out of use by 1914, but the UNDERGROUND wordmark persisted for considerably longer.

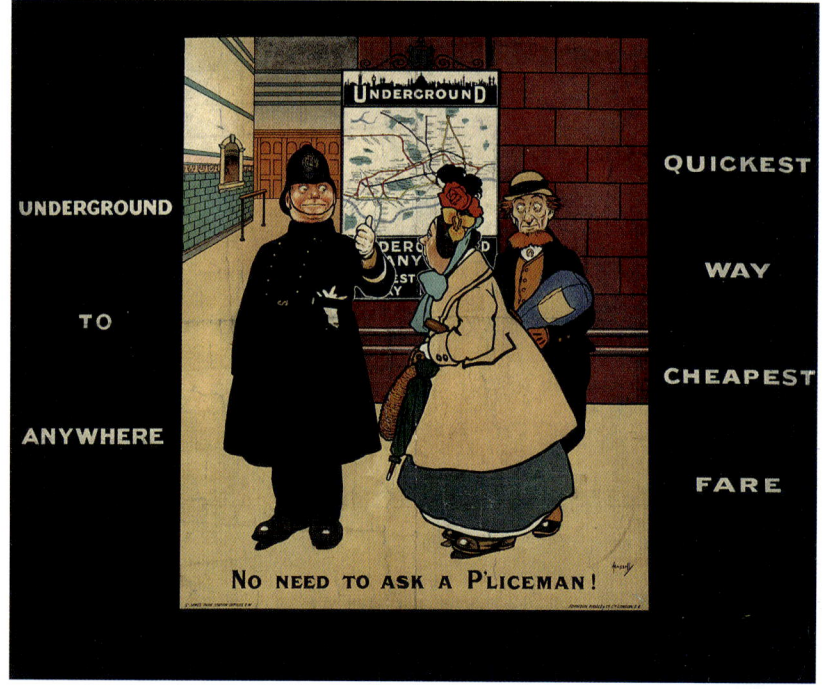

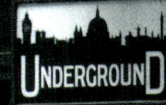
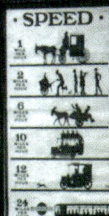
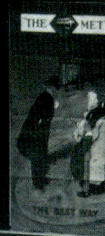
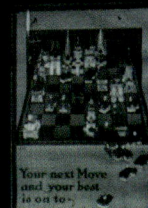

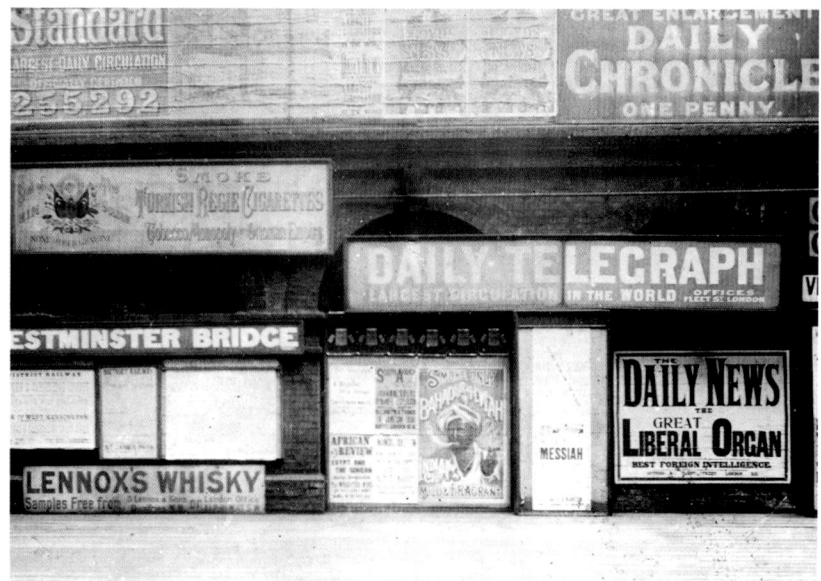

The problem Frank Pick inherited: Victorian advertising overwhelming station signage, seen here in an 1896 photograph of Westminster Bridge station (later renamed Westminster) on the Metropolitan District Railway (which became the District Line after 1933).

simply as 'London Transport'. Under their leadership, innovative developments in public transport were to transform the everyday rhythms of life in the capital, as well as its appearance and its growth.

An immediate objective was to drive up fare income, especially in the off-peak hours when the system tended to be under-used. The Underground needed to attract more passengers as well as repeat business, and this was to be achieved by publicising it more effectively, making its stations easier to identify, and rendering the system easier to use and to navigate. In the long term some of these improvements would be achieved through significant capital investment, but at the time of the initial cash crisis cheaper and quicker solutions were needed.

Pick's first initiative, and one which continues to the present, was for the Underground to commission leading poster artists of the day to produce imaginative and modern campaigns to both 'brand' and encourage use of the system. At the same time, he and Stanley were concerned with improving what is now called 'wayfinding' – smoothing and simplifying passengers' journeys through the

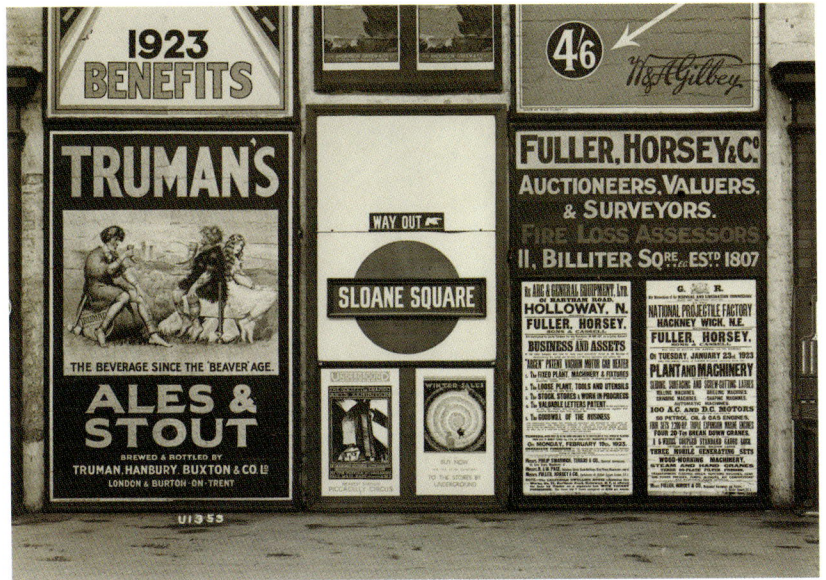

Evidence of Pick's early attempts to curb the 'graphic noise' of wall-to-wall advertising, seen here at Sloane Square station on the District Railway in 1923: a cleared white space to display the station name board, backed by a solid red disc for emphasis.

system. As Oliver Green observes, 'Pick was very conscious of how alienating and overwhelming a vast city like London could be. It was difficult to take in and comprehend, as he recalled from his first trip to the capital from York as a schoolboy.'[41] So he decided to enlist Johnston's help in implementing one of the world's first corporate identity exercises – not that either Pick or Johnston would have recognised that description of their work.

Pick was particularly concerned to make stations and station names stand out against the 'graphic noise' caused by the large amounts of advertising displayed throughout the system. The revenue this generated was vital, so removing advertisements was not an option. However, Pick managed to persuade Stanley that 'fewer advertisements well-spaced out and displayed in an orderly fashion would bring in twice as much revenue as the old method of filling every available space with a mass of different shapes and sizes'.[42] Into these newly cleared spaces at station entrances Pick installed a standard logotype – the word UNDERGROUND with enlarged initial and terminal letters. At platform level the spaces were used to display the station name in white sans-serif 'grotesque' lettering on

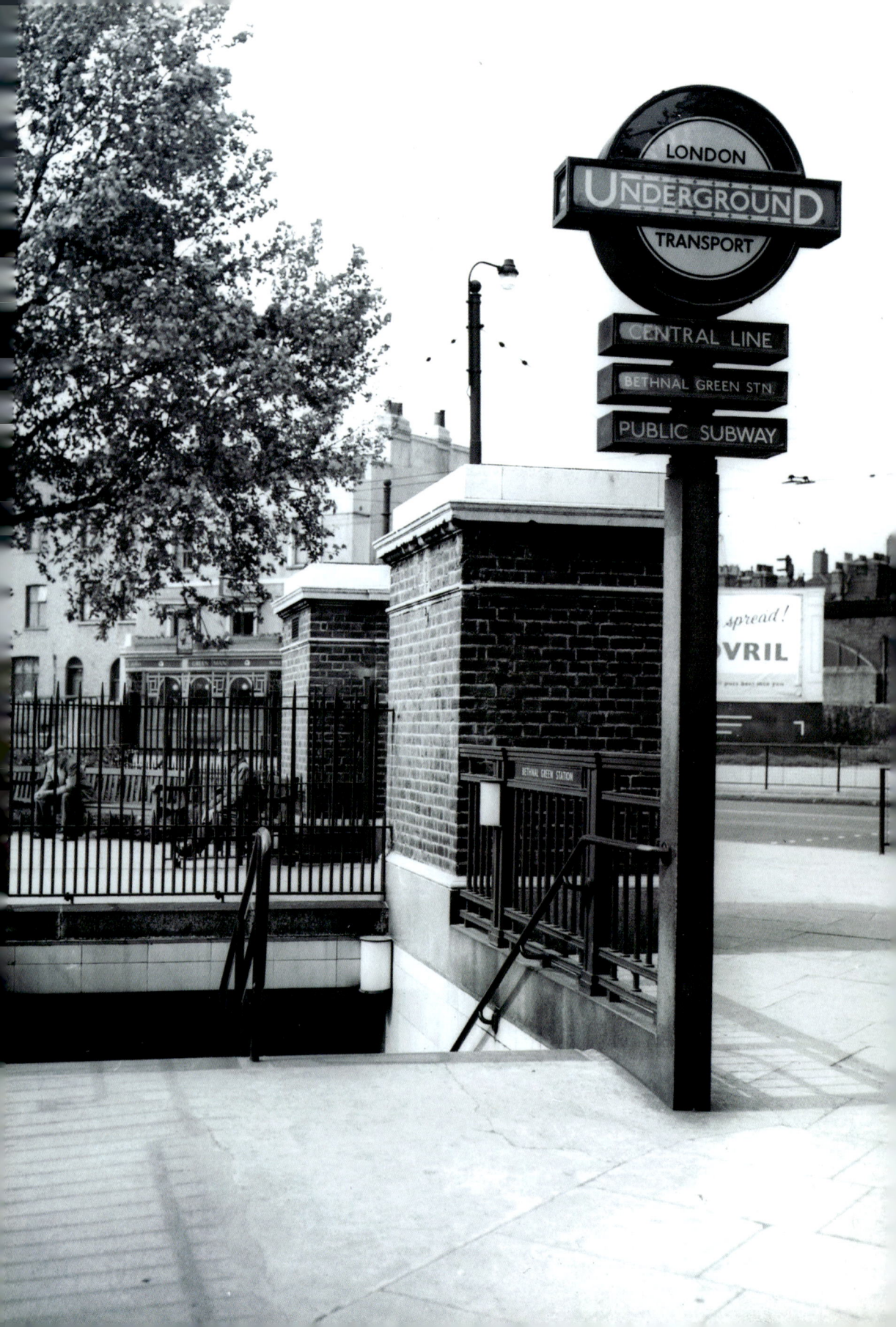

JOHNSTON AND LONDON

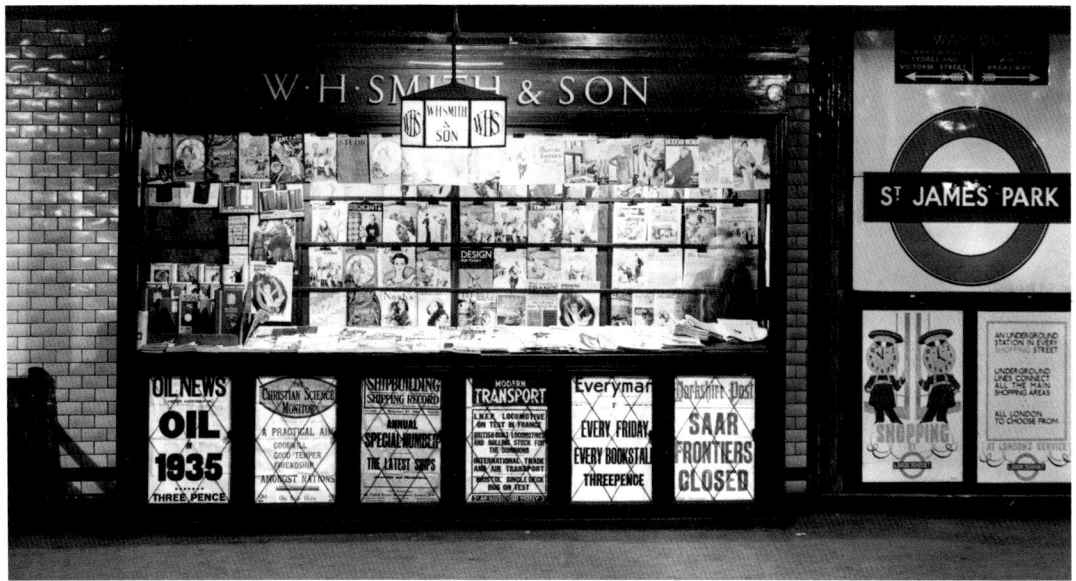

One of the many W.H. Smith bookstalls scattered through the Underground network, photographed at St James Park station in 1935. Although impressed by Eric Gill's lettering for the business's name (in a style based on letter-cutting in stone), Frank Pick thought it unsuitable for station signage, preferring sans-serif block lettering with a more modern feel.

a blue background, the nameboards then being backed by a solid red disc to make them stand out even more.

These experiments using generic block lettering seem to have prompted Pick to the realisation that what the Underground needed was its own distinctive and unique lettering style. This was to form the basis of his discussions with Edward Johnston from 1913 onwards. The conversations were brokered by Gerard Meynell, the only person whom Johnston trusted to look after his interests in commercial business dealings.[43]

Pick required a lettering style which would 'belong unmistakably to the times in which we lived'; and which would have 'the bold simplicity of the authentic lettering of the best periods and yet belong unmistakably to the twentieth century'. Vitally, the alphabet must have 'the character of an official railway sign that was not to be mistaken by people in a hurry for a trader's advertisement'.[44] Pick had admired Eric Gill's painted lettering (of 1904) for W. H. Smith & Sons (roman capitals based on those on Trajan's Column in Rome), but Smith's bookstalls were

Opposite An example of the style of signage introduced as a result of the recommendations for standardisation in the *Carr-Edwards Report* (1938), probably installed after the Second World War and seen here at Bethnal Green in 1955.

already a popular feature of Underground stations. Pick wished to use a distinctly different style, and so made his only prescribed condition for the commission that the letters be block-letter monostroke, in other words that all strokes making up the letters be of the same thickness.[45]

After their initial meeting in 1913, Pick and Johnston did not meet again until 29th October 1915, this time with Eric Gill as well as Meynell present. It was at this meeting, where they 'discussed blockletters' for the first time, that Pick asked Gill and Johnston to think about working on the project together.

Ten days later, on 8th November, Johnston met Pick and Meynell, this time without Gill, and promised that by mid December he would give Pick 'two or three alphabets' for an agreed fee of fifty guineas. Eric Gill's diary records that the previous day he had met Johnston and Douglas Pepler for tea, and that they had discussed Pick's requirements. It was presumably then that Gill announced that he would have to drop out of the job because he was already fully occupied in carving the Stations of the Cross for Westminster Cathedral. Even so, Johnston later passed ten per cent of his fee to Gill in recognition of his contribution.

The two original hand-drawn sets of designs for block letters presented by Edward Johnston to Frank Pick in June (uppercase) and July 1916 (lowercase and numerals). Note the uppercase crossed W which was used in some contexts for only a few years before being abandoned in favour of the more conventional W, and the variants of lowercase a, g and q. Johnston's background as a calligrapher is clear in the chisel-shaped top of the figure 1 and the diamond-shaped dots on the i and the j.

Johnston's first sketches reveal that he was initially thinking in terms of monoline 'petit-serif' lettering.[46] It was presumably when he showed these drafts for the capitals O B D E U and N to Pick in December 1915 that the 'petit-serif' idea was dropped. That Johnston would not meet his December deadline for 'two or three alphabets' was already clear. Johnston started work on the alphabet in earnest in January 1916, and it took most of that year for both upper and lower case to be completed. In fact, in November 1916 Pick noticed that the final lower-case drawings lacked an 'f', which Johnston quickly drew and sent back, accompanied by a note explaining that he had been much preoccupied with buying a house (Halletts Farm).

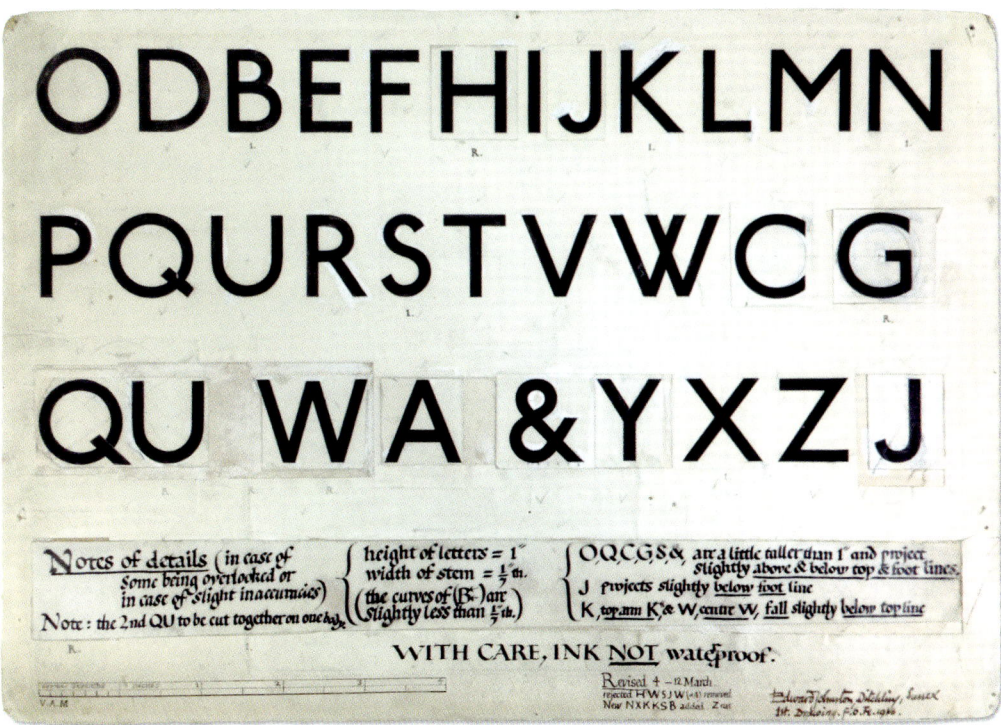

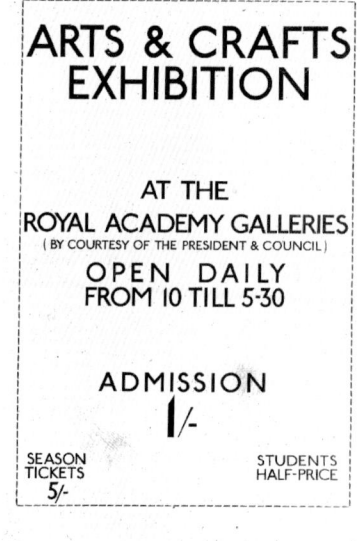
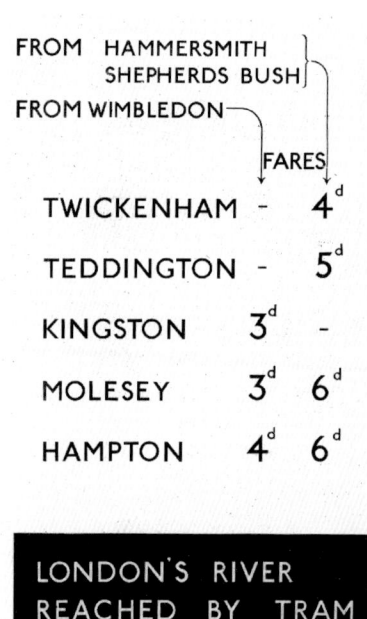

Two of the earliest posters using Johnston lettering, dating from November (left) and July 1916 (right). Both predate the manufacture of movable Johnston type: the lettering was handcopied for lithographic reproduction.

Opposite Wood and metal Johnston type was manufactured by Stephenson Blake of Sheffield from 1917, although from 1940 onwards wooden type (as illustrated here) was entirely subcontracted to Robert De Little of York. Cases were retained by all printers who worked for UERL on the strict understanding that the type was to be used exclusively for London Underground jobs.

Of the finished product, Nikolaus Pevsner wrote:

> When at last it was ready in the summer of 1916 (in capitals as well as lower case), it was far more harmonious and balanced than Pick can have visualized during the preparatory stages – a truly twentieth century Sans, logical and consistent, based as far as possible on squares and circles and thus of convincing and restful proportions ...[47]

The capital letter O was identified by Johnston as the key letter, and is a perfect circle. The capital M is a square, with the diagonals meeting precisely in the centre of the square. Legibility was Johnston's principal objective, but he made light of his months of painstaking labour by claiming that he had simply gone back to classical Roman capitals for the proportions. 'Once this basis had been established', writes Priscilla Johnston, ' "the alphabet", in his own words, "designed itself." ' [48]

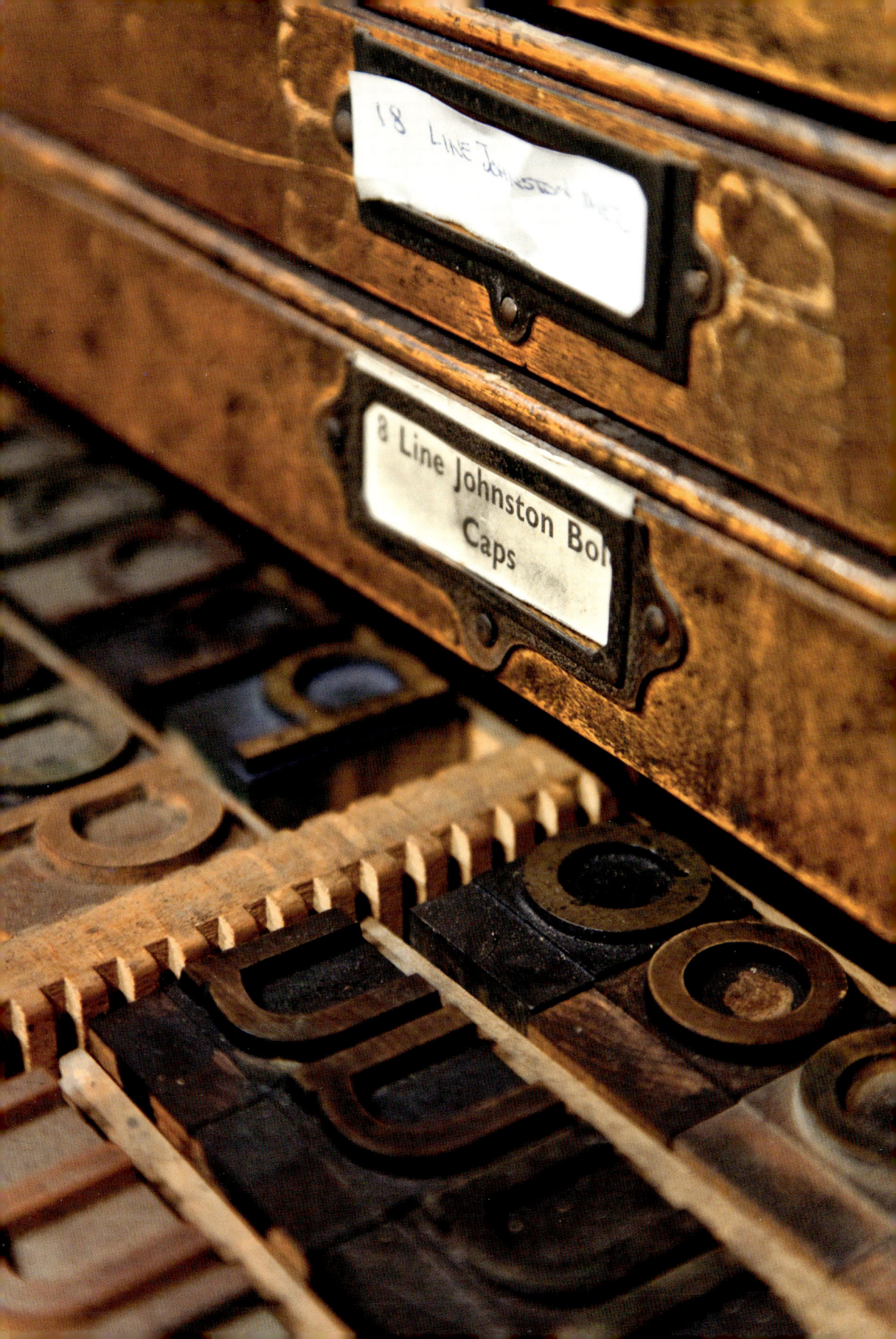

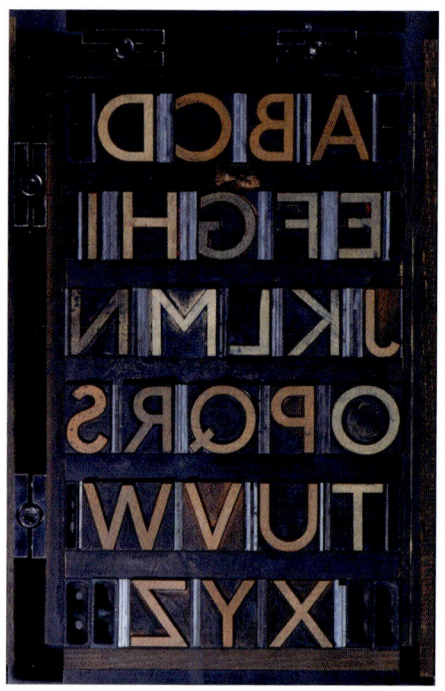
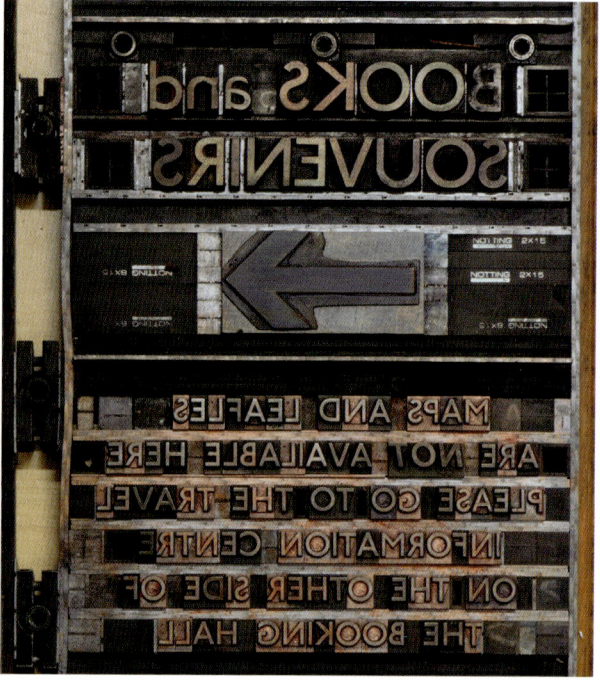

Above Part of a full alphabet set of Johnston wood type. Spacing movable type elegantly was always challenging and depended on the individual skills of the compositor. This task had to be done by eye using varying widths of letter-spacing material as seen here between the wood letter blocks.

Right Johnston metal type 'locked up' in a chase.

The new alphabet was put to immediate use, with text posters being produced in the summer and autumn of 1916 to advertise the Arts and Crafts Exhibition at Burlington House and – more prosaically – tram fares for day trips to the river from Hammersmith, Shepherd's Bush and Wimbledon. These early posters were produced lithographically, with the letterforms being re-drawn from Johnston's original designs. Johnston had nothing to do with the process by which the wood and metal type was cut for his new alphabet, and it appears that it was not until late 1921 that full fount sets of wooden and metal type in a variety of sizes were available for use by UERL's printers.

The new fount – increasingly known as 'Johnston Sans' – was the private property of UERL. Printers working on Underground contracts were expressly forbidden to use their cabinets of Johnston Sans for any other clients. This created a gap in the market for a commercially available modern sans-serif block letter: hence the immediate popularity of Monotype's Gill Sans face when it

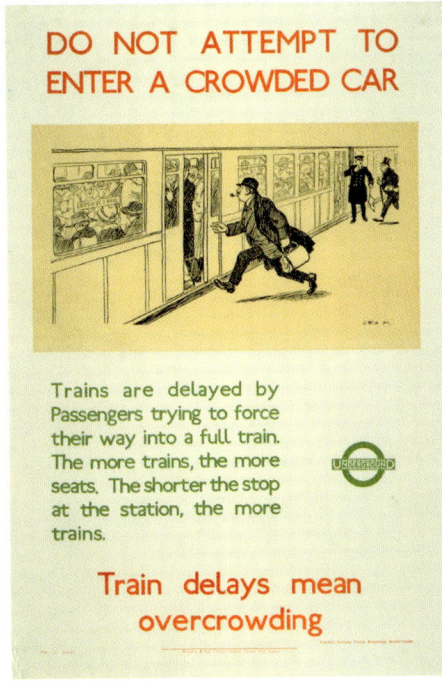 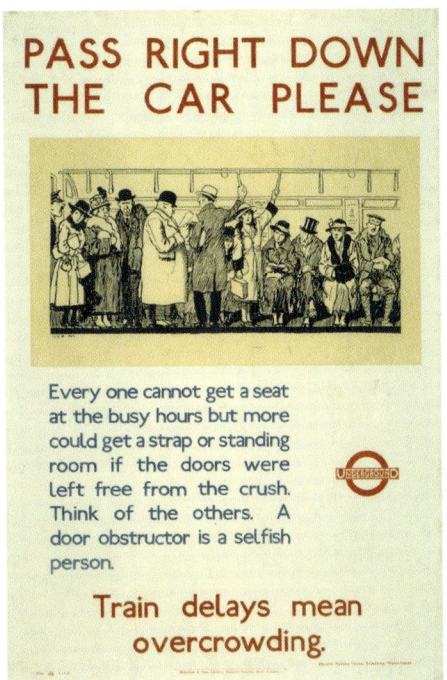

was released in 1928, in a wide range of weights. This in turn prompted the Underground in the late 1920s to commission a new bold version of Johnston Sans. (Unlike modern digital typefaces, which are designed from the outset in a range of weights, sizes and degrees of compression, the original Johnston Sans was only ever available in a restricted range of sizes and just two weights.)

One issue with the new typeface was the question of spacing. There seems to have been a misguided feeling that an important benefit of Johnston Sans was that it could be set tightly to save space, and early posters often show the erratic and irregular results. In fact, set correctly, Johnston Sans is a comparatively wide type, and Johnston himself was aware that good letter spacing was crucial, comparing it to the packing of eggs: '[the letters should be] as close as they can be put – tightly fitted without breakages'.[49] Even so, spacing continued to present a challenge until the 1980s, when first photo-typesetting and then digital tools finally allowed it to be automatically calibrated.

George Morrow's humorous (and still relevant) posters from 1918, advising passengers on Underground etiquette, are very early examples of the use of Johnston Sans type in both uppercase and lowercase. Close examination of the lowercase text reveals that the UERL's printers had not yet got to grips with the challenge of spacing the new typeface correctly.

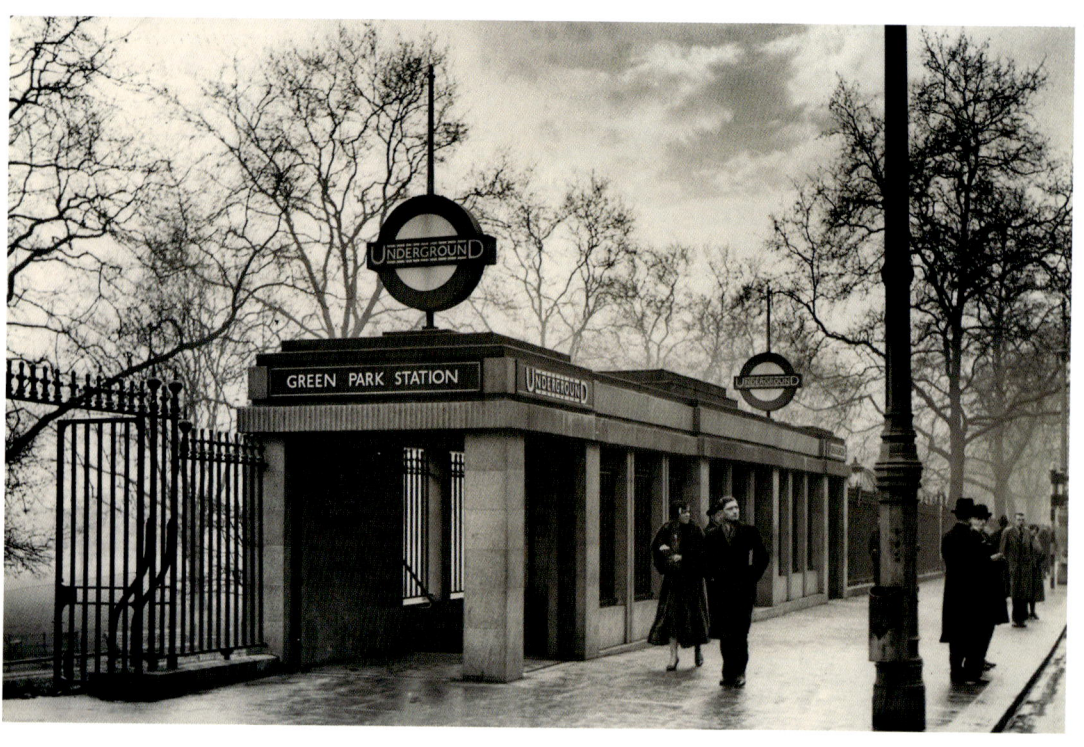

Entrance on Piccadilly to Green Park Undergound station designed by Charles Holden, built in Portland stone (1932), and showing Holden's integration of Johnston signage into his UERL structures. It remained in use until 1971 when it was demolished to make way for a new ventilator block.

It seems that originally Johnston had no thought of his new lettering being used extensively for signage (as opposed to posters). It is a tribute to the adaptability and robustness of his design that Johnston Sans is routinely hailed as an exemplar face for public lettering. The new alphabet spread across the system slowly, being deployed only when existing signs needed to be replaced. In 1924-25, the Underground Group allowed it to be used for notices at the British Empire Exhibition at Wembley, but otherwise the Standard Alphabet was not widely seen across the capital until the mid 1920s when architect Charles Holden started work on major extensions to the Underground network and Johnston Sans was specified for all new signage.

The question of signage brings us to what is probably Johnston's best-known work for the Underground: the bullseye logotype (later renamed the 'roundel'). There is little surviving evidence for the design process that led to its creation. Pick first asked Johnston

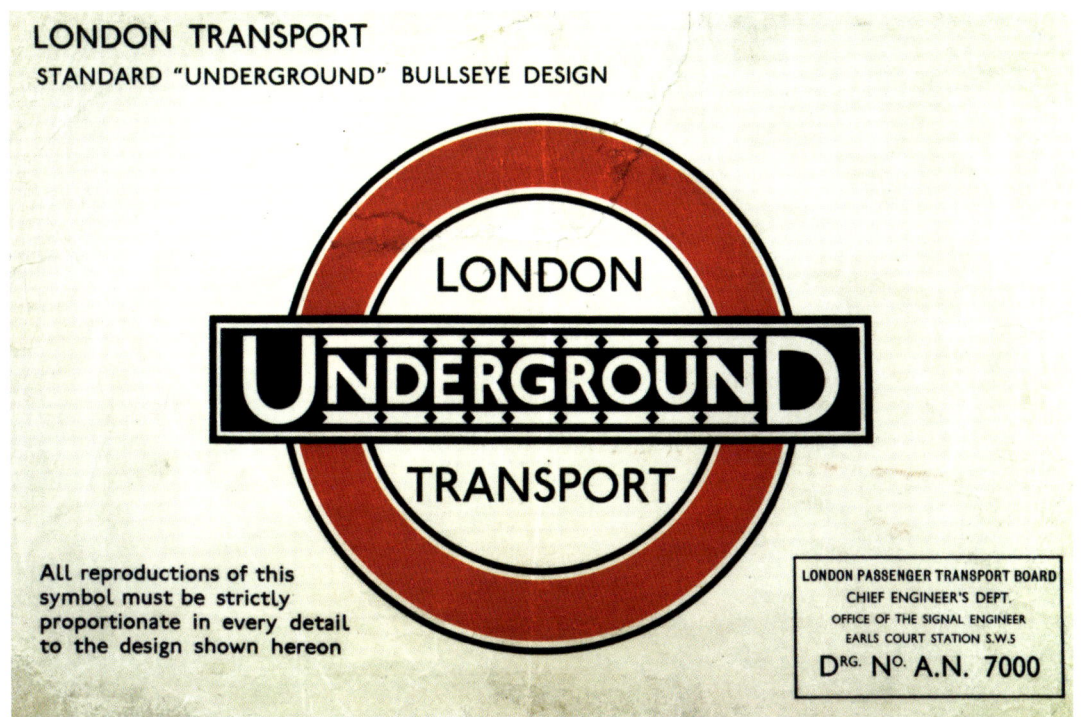

One of Johnston's final jobs for Frank Pick: the post-1933 adaption of his UNDERGROUND bullseye to form the logo for the new London Passenger Transport Board. The first proposal had the initials L.P.T.B. in the upper counter (the enclosed white space), but Lord Ashfield preferred this more balanced design with the company's trading name, London Transport, split between both counters.

around 1916 or 1917 to review the trading marks used by the Underground Group, as a natural extension of his work on the new alphabet. As reconstructed by Justin Howes, what seems to have happened is that Johnston first attempted to streamline the established UNDERGROUND logotype, maintaining the existing style of capitalised initial and terminal letters but with the hyphens above and below the intermediate letters joined up into a continuous band.[50] This did not find favour, and so by mid 1917 Johnston had produced a label with UNDERGROUND reversed out of a coloured background and with the intermediate letters bordered above and below by bands which Johnston called 'ribbons'. These were pierced at the spaces between the letters with the same diamond-shaped points he had used as the full stops in his new typeface.

During the Great War, the Young Men's Christian Association (YMCA) logo of a bar superimposed on a triangle was a common sight on refreshment stalls and the like (*see* page 47). Inspired by this,

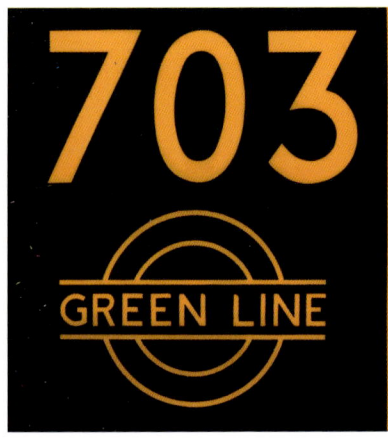

Late examples of hand craftsmanship in London Transport signage. Until the 1960s LT bus and coach destination roller blinds were produced by pasting individual silk-screen-printed paper labels on a linen roll. These Green Line examples show the change from using only capitals before 1961 to the use of upper- and lower-case letters after 1961, all based on Johnston's compressed bus letters.

Pick suggested Johnston use something like it but 'more balanced', and sketched an idea of a ring rather than the existing Underground solid disc.[51] Between 1917 and 1920 Johnston worked on making subtle alterations to the proportions of the symbol: increasing the white spaces inside the red circle, re-drawing the lettering to a heavier weight, balancing the bar so that only the initial U and terminal D hung outside the circle, and adding subtle ledger lines both inside and outside the circle.

The resulting logotype provided the basis for multiple adaptions with which to brand all modes of transport provided by the Underground Group. In 1933 it was easily modified to become the corporate symbol of the new London Transport organisation. In subsequent decades the device has come to stand as symbol not just for public transport in London, but for the city itself: in David Lawrence's words, it is 'a logo for London'.

To complete the story we must also mention Johnston's third and final piece of graphic innovation for Frank Pick. This comprised a condensed alphabet for the destination boards of the Underground's subsidiary, the London General Omnibus Company, designed between 1919 and 1922. The challenge was that police regulations required a certain size of letter, but bus boards had to carry so much information about stopping points that in many cases the squashed-together words were unreadable from a distance. The story is told by Priscilla Johnston of her father spending spare time on his Mondays in London standing by the kerb studying buses as they came towards him so as to observe the legibility problems, and having his work constantly interrupted by well-meaning passers-by who would take pity on the 'obvious countryman' with the 'lost look in his eyes, stranded on the pavement's edge' and try to help him on his way.[52]

Johnston's solution was to calculate mathematically a condensed version of his sans-serif railway block-lettering in order to fit in the necessary number of letters. He then made ingenious alterations to the letterforms (for example, raising the bowl of the 'R') to preserve legibility. It is these alterations that make Johnston's bus lettering more than a simple mechanical compression of his original type. In the bus lettering Johnston slightly thinned the monoline strokes where they meet so as to preserve the optical illusion that all strokes are of the same width. (He had not done this with his railway Standard Alphabet, one of the quirks which gives the latter much of its character, but which also makes it a slightly awkward letterform to read in anything other than a large display face.) Nonetheless, Johnston's bus lettering was the first of his styles to be replaced. Following numerous in-house legibility trials, London Transport decided from 1961 to introduce lower-case letters on destination blinds, and Johnston's Omnibus alphabets were significantly redesigned in a new lighter weight style, albeit one clearly based on the original.[53]

After this initial astonishing burst of creativity, much of Johnston's work for Frank Pick, from the mid 1920s, involved acting as what would now be called a 'design consultant.' This role proved to be far more remunerative for Johnston: for example, in December 1933 he received £78 15s for preparing reports on various labels and signs (which were described by Justin Howes as 'extraordinarily thorough'), compared with the fifty guineas (shared with Gill) he received for a year's work designing Johnston Sans in 1916.[54]

Johnston was, and for all his life remained, primarily a calligrapher, but there was little place for that talent to be exercised in the Underground. However one opportunity did present itself.[55] In 1920, Johnston was commissioned by Henry Carr, the Assistant Publicity Officer for the Underground Group, to produce a set of calligraphic cyphers of the initials of the Underground's subsidiary railway companies. These were to be 'engraved on a small silver circle ... and placed on top of a picture frame with silver corners' designed for best-kept station competition diplomas. Johnston duly produced the designs, but it is not clear whether they were ever used.

The cyphers were followed by three pen-drawn borders for posters, probably executed in November 1922. These were, as Justin Howes puts it, 'a very Johnstonian invention', based on his belief that the decoration of a manuscript should be produced using the same broad-edged pen as that used for writing the text. The borders appeared on a handful of text posters issued in January and February 1923 but were not otherwise adopted. In a letter to

An example of a border design by Edward Johnston, 1923. The original was drawn in pen and ink.

TAKE RETURN TICKETS TO L.N.W. STATIONS

Return tickets are now issued from this station to the following points on the L. N. W. Railway:

Kenton	Bushey & Oxhey
Harrow & Wealdstone	Watford (High Street)
Stanmore	Watford Junction
Headstone Lane	Watford West
Hatch End (for Pinner)	Rickmansworth
Carpender's Park	Croxley Green

SAVE TIME AND TROUBLE

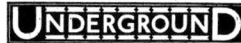

Johnston in February 1923, Henry Carr mentioned the borders: 'In passing, we would say that in our opinion something definite should be arranged for turning the corners. At the present time the two vertical borders look very unfinished.' For some reason Johnston never equipped his designs for the Underground with corners, although he did draw some in 1929 for Gerard Meynell.

Johnston's penultimate work of penmanship for the Underground was a doodle of a monogram for the newly created London Passenger Transport Board (LPTB), produced in April 1933 but not further developed. Rather appropriately, his last public commission of any kind – not just for London Transport – was for a calligraphic inscription on a blotter to be presented to Frank Pick as a retirement gift in 1940. After a long career, Pick's departure was sad and rather awkward. He had disagreed with other members of the LPT Board over government proposals to limit LPTB dividends, and (taking what seems to have been a calculated risk) stated his intention to retire from the board at the end of his term in May 1940. He seems to have hoped to continue with the LPTB as general manager, but Ashfield called his bluff and chose not to find him such a position. So, to many people's surprise, Pick retired on 18th May 1940, officially due to failing health. (The ostensible reason may not have been entirely incorrect as he died the following year at the early age of 62.)

Johnston is reported to have made an exceptional effort with the blotter because it was for Frank Pick, and the inscription is rendered in his characteristic late style using large cypher capitals. This work stands as a tribute to the personal and professional relationship between the two men, and as an appropriate coda to a lifetime of work with lettering, principally for London's Underground system. Justin Howes, writing in 2000, believed the blotter to have been mislaid in 1945, so it is pleasing to report that it is actually safely housed in the collections of the London Transport Museum.[56]

Detail from the blotter presented to Frank Pick on his retirement in 1940 with a calligraphic inscription by Johnston followed by the signatures of Pick's colleagues, headed by Lord Ashfield.

JP

Your many friends offer this small token of their affection & esteem

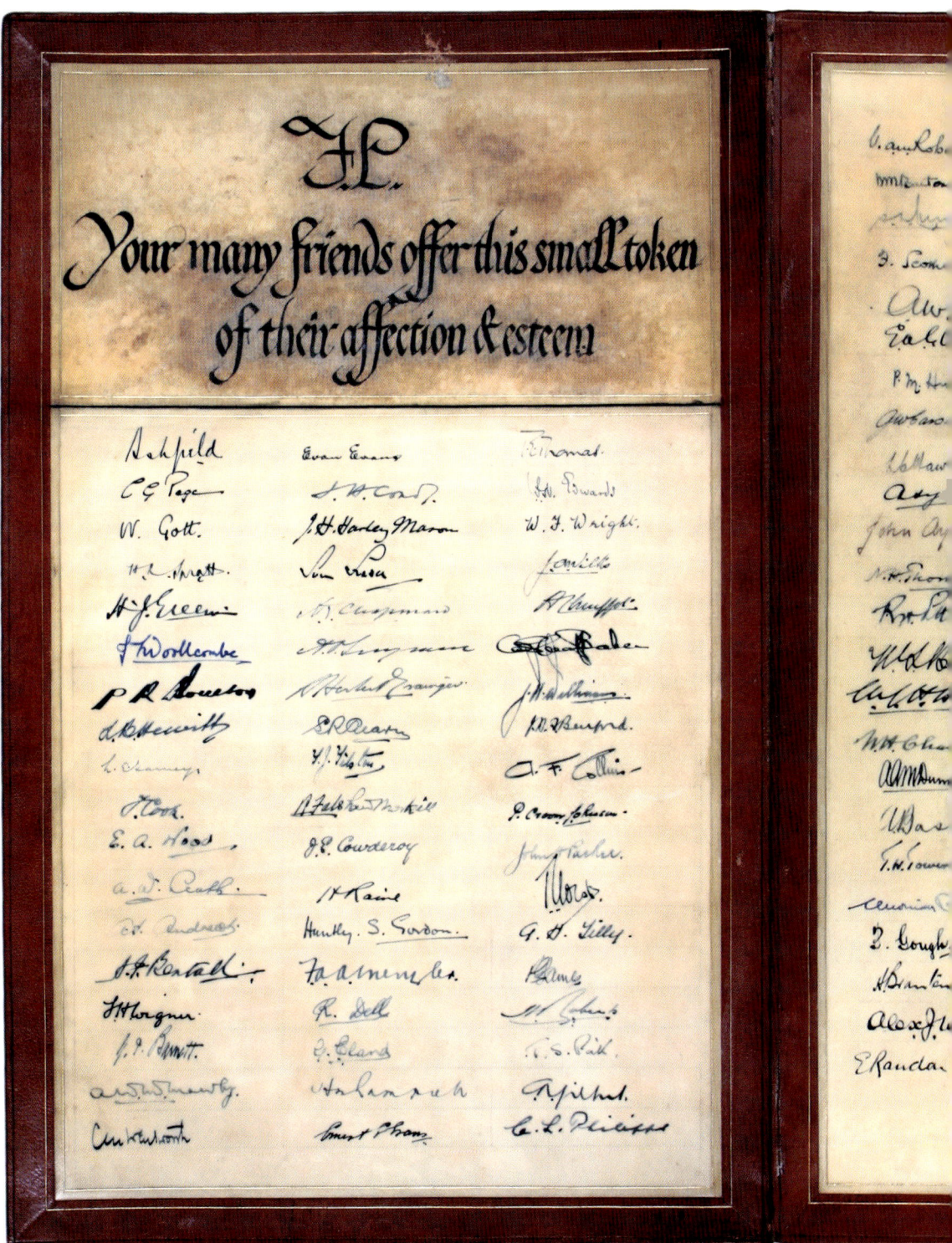

ABCDE
FGHIJK
LMNOP
QRSTU
VXY.&,W Z

POSTSCRIPT: JOHNSTON AFTER JOHNSTON

Typography has one plain duty and that is to convey information in writing. Emil Ruder (1914-70)

The great strength of Johnston's work for the Underground Group, as passed on to its successors London Transport and now Transport for London (TfL), is its adaptability to changing circumstances and times. Even before Johnston's retirement, the development of his block lettering and the bullseye were passing out of his hands. Percy Delf Smith, one of Johnston's pupils, collaborated with Charles Holden in 1930-31 to design a petit-serif alphabet based on Johnston's block letters but with 'the proportions ... varied somewhat.'[57] This new alphabet was intended for the signage in the new UERL headquarters building at 55 Broadway, SW1, but was also used by Holden at a few stations on the Piccadilly Line extensions then under construction. The reason for this commission is not clear: perhaps Pick was concerned that Johnston's painstaking pace of work would not be compatible with the planned rapid expansion of the network, or might he have been looking to move on to a new generation of lettering artists? Whatever the reason, the Delf Smith petit serifs did not spread widely, and the signs can today be seen only at Sudbury Town station (Piccadilly Line) and in the London Transport Museum collection.[58]

Percy Delf Smith's petit-serif alphabet illustrated in *Civic and Memorial Lettering*, 1946.

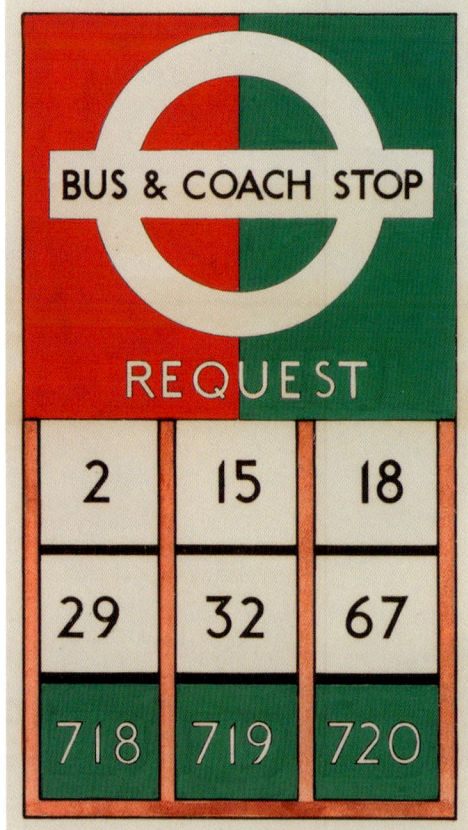

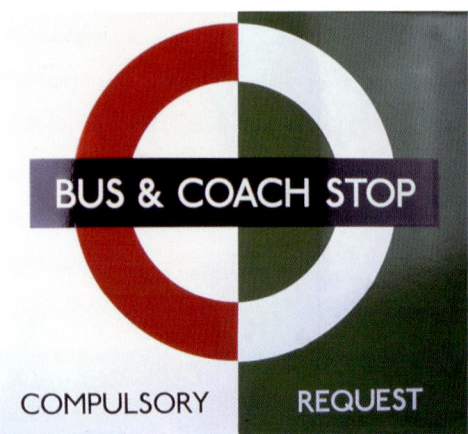

Hans Schleger's redesigned solid bullseye for road service stop flags as introduced from 1935: (right) for a single service, and (left) adapted to allow one flag to display two services.

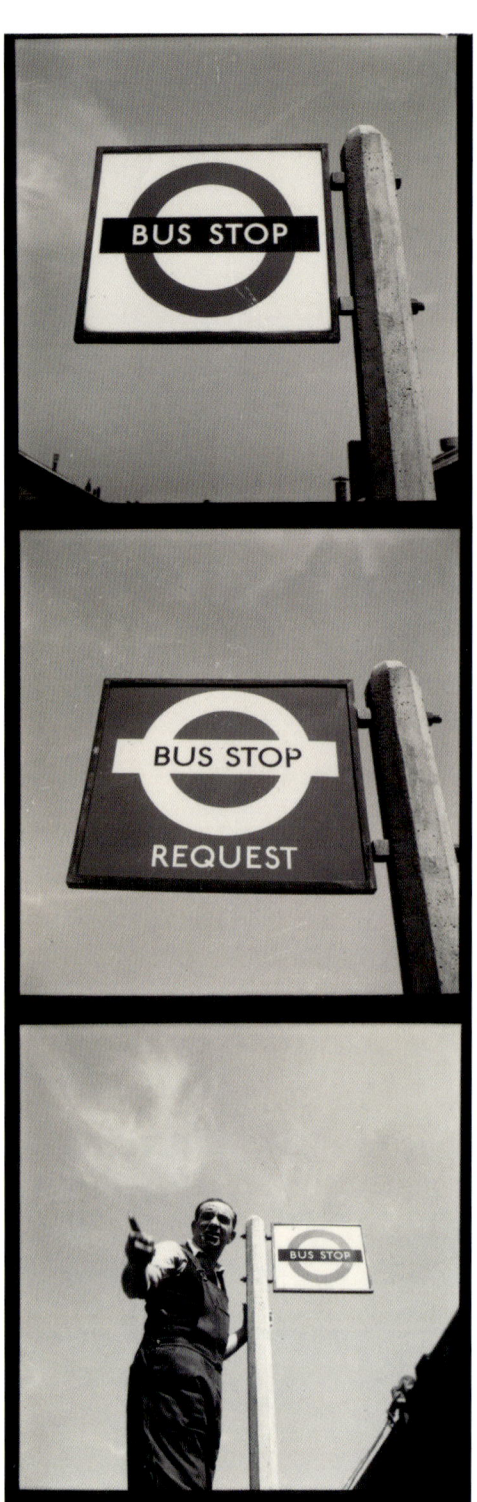

In 1935 the graphic designer Hans Schleger (who worked under the name 'Zero') was asked to re-design the bullseye as a result of the decision to abandon the original custom of allowing passengers to hail road vehicle services at will and to create instead a system-wide scheme of fixed stopping places for buses, trams, trolleybuses and coaches. Schleger's new scheme was based on a plain single-colour bar and circle in both silhouette and outline form, colour-coded for the different types of services: red for buses, green for coaches and blue for trams. This revision showed that the bullseye symbol was already so well known that even without lettering it was understood to represent the whole London transport system.

In 1938 these efforts to produce a consistent branding scheme were taken a step further with the production of the *Carr-Edwards Report*. Put together by W. P. N. Edwards (Lord Ashfield's secretary) and Publicity Officer Henry Carr, the report concentrated on 'the standards which should, in our opinion, be adopted governing the location and types of direction signs, notices and maps upon the railways'; it was intended to bring some order to the signage requirements of the planned New Works Programme (from 1935) of Underground expansion.[59]

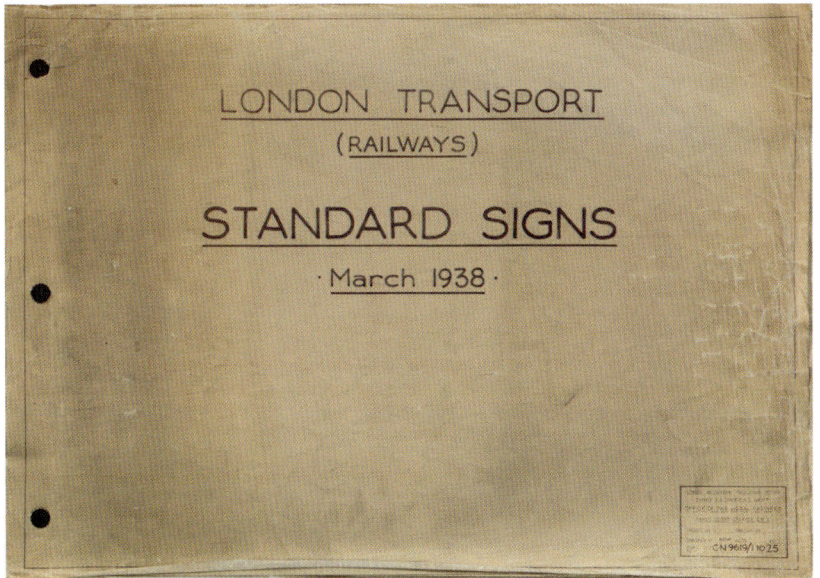

Cover of the first *Standard Signs* manual for London Transport, produced in 1938 as part of the *Carr-Edwards Report*.

Overleaf Examples of designs from the manual showing, among other things, the directional arrow (not a Johnston design) finally standardised with three flights: previously arrows had appeared with two, four or even five flights as well as three.

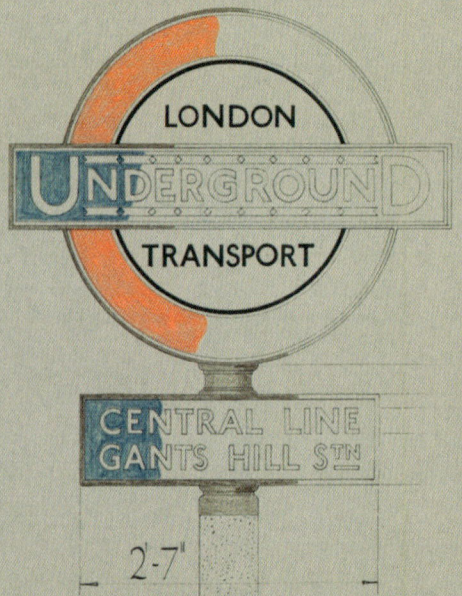
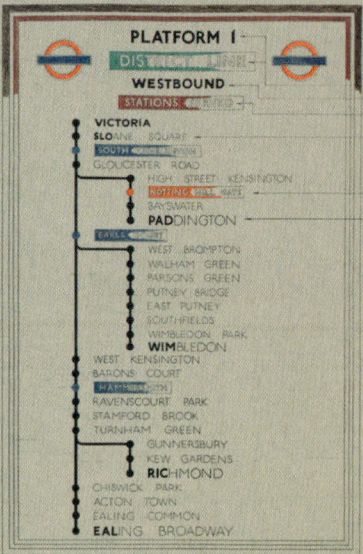
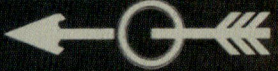
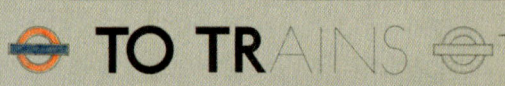
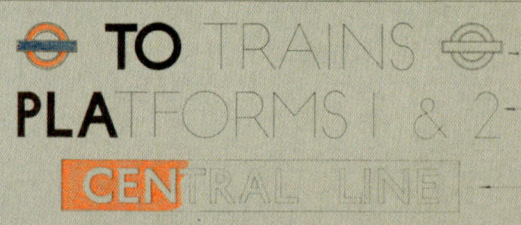
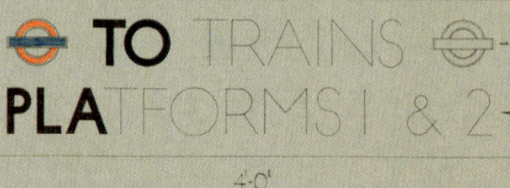
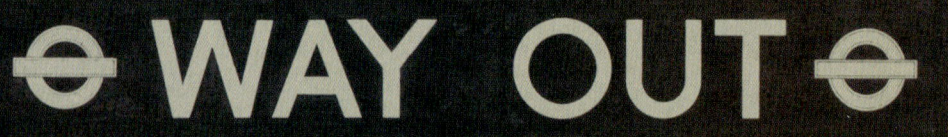

Colours are not permitted for
illuminated signs on station platforms
Coloured Bullseyes & Line colours to be used elsewhere.

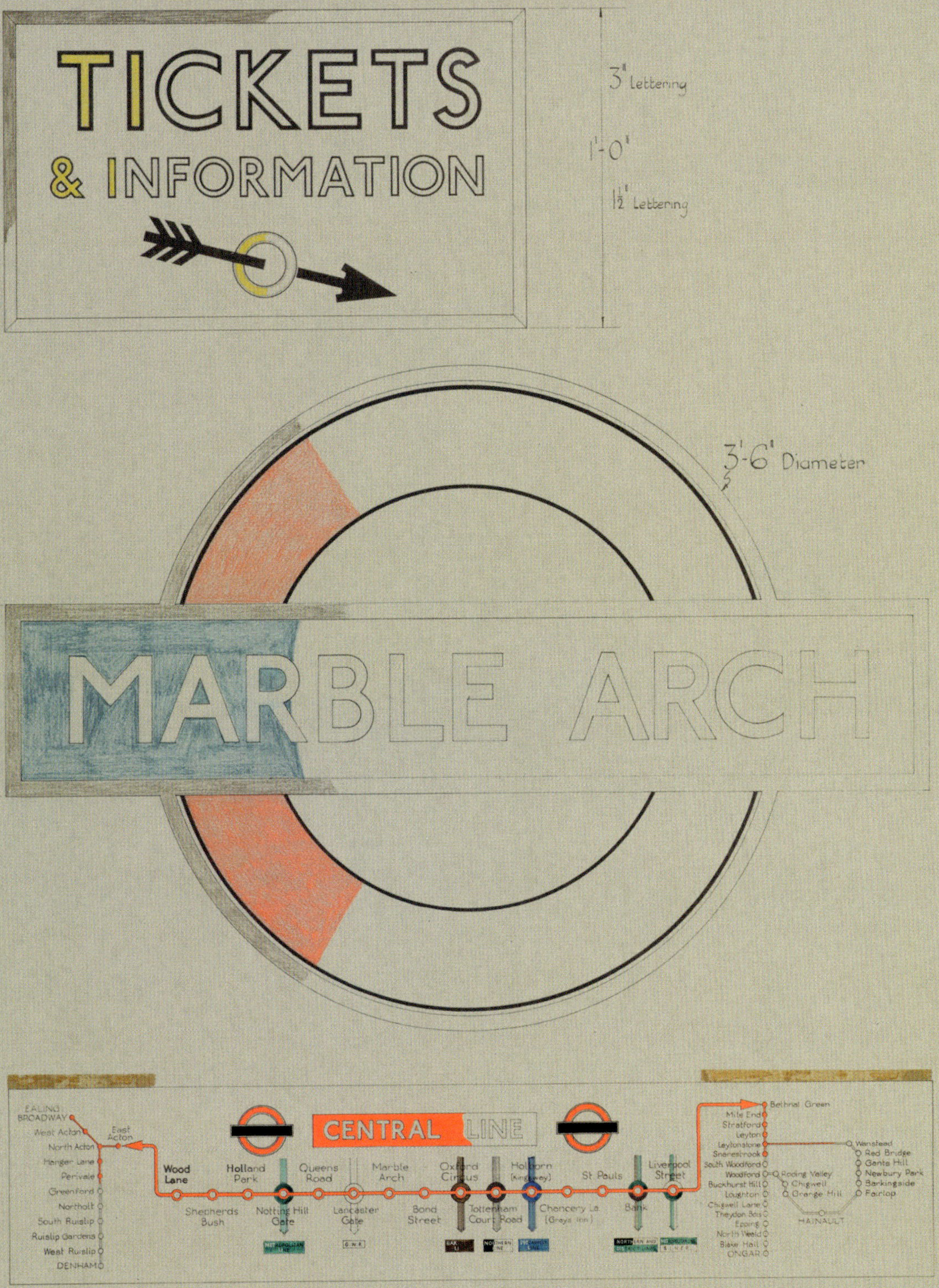

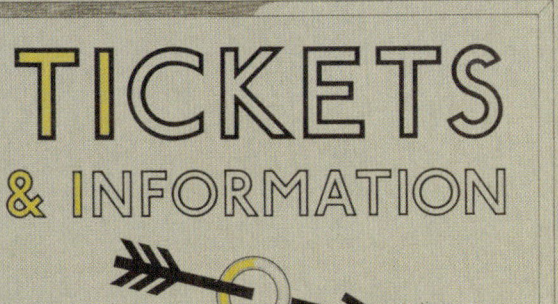

3" lettering
1'-0"
1½" lettering

3'-6" Diameter

MARBLE ARCH

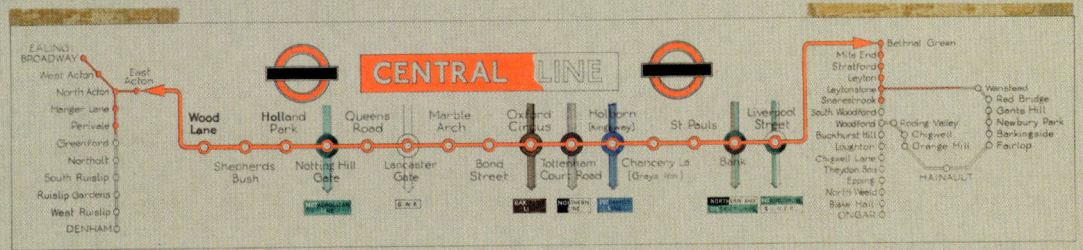

The *Carr-Edwards Report* and its accompanying drawings arguably represented the first attempt to compile a manual of graphic standards for an organisation, certainly for any transport organisation. It recommended the installation of Underground bullseyes outside each station, and the use of bullseyes on all signs and notices related to the transport system, while recognising that 'complete standardisation of signs is unfortunately impossible without a standard design of station'. Its full implementation had to wait until after the Second World War, at which point austerity measures meant that some of its recommendations had to be reined in. However it is worth nothing that this report was the first in a series of London Transport and TfL corporate design manuals which have continued to appear to the present day.

By the time that inland public transport was nationalised in 1948, Johnston's work had lost its original champions. Pick and Johnston both died during the war, Henry Carr retired in 1946 and Lord Ashfield retired in 1947 (and died in 1948). In 1947, following a period of several years when the post had been vacant, London Transport appointed Harold Hutchison, a former Creative Head at Unilever, as the new Publicity Officer. Brian Webb writes that 'Hutchison's first task was to restore public confidence in the capital's transport system … [but] he was equally aware of the urgent need to raise revenue through encouraging leisure travel', and the pace of change accelerated.[60] Hutchison regarded the Johnston ribboned Underground logo as 'a disaster – a sad lapse' and in 1947 ordered its redesign with equal height lettering and the dashes removed.[61] The gradual replacement of the Underground branding on the bullseye with London Transport, started by Ashfield and Schleger, was accelerated by Hutchison. However, only a few years later this process was halted by Sir John Elliott after his appointment as chair of London Transport in 1953.

Throughout the 1950s and 1960s the bullseye device was subjected to competing attempts to modify it or ornament it according to

POSTSCRIPT: JOHNSTON AFTER JOHNSTON

the whims of individual designers. At the same time Johnston Sans was facing competition on posters and printed materials from other typefaces such as Gill Sans and Univers which were seen as more 'modern' and were certainly more flexible. However, Hutchison did commission a new lighter weight of Johnston to be used on illuminated signs.

In the mid 1960s, Misha Black's Design Research Unit (DRU) consultancy was appointed to produce all graphics and signage for the new Victoria Line. DRU's recommendations for a stripped-back scheme led to them being commissioned in 1971 to review the whole of London Transport's signage systems. Picking up on the proliferation of patriotic symbols on tourist goods in 1960s, Black remarked caustically that the historical use of the bullseye 'in a variety of forms, inconsistencies of shape, repetitively as borders to printed material and with humorous connotations, is as inappropriate as a girl's Union Jack printed pants.' DRU redrew the bullseye with altered proportions and renamed it 'the roundel', to be used in a restricted palette of colours without any text the intention being for it to work in much the same way that 'the Queen's head on a stamp … makes the name of the country redundant.' [62] DRU's recommendations for the roundel were never fully adopted owing to resistance from individual business units within London Transport. But the concept of the 'universal roundel' has taken on new life in the 21st century with Transport for London's expansion into managing new modes of public transport. All of TfL's new responsibilities – bicycles, taxis, light rail, the Overground and even the Greenwich cable car – have their own variant on the roundel, individually colour-coded but identifying them collectively as part of a single transport system.

DRU was entirely positive about the Johnston Sans typeface, but the problem of the restricted range of weights and sizes available in Johnston metal and wooden type remained, and in 1973 the type designer Walter Tracy was asked to review the continued use

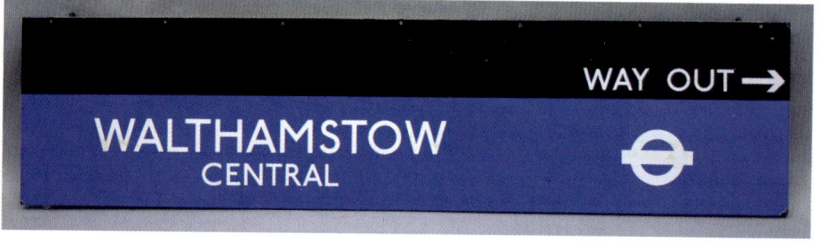

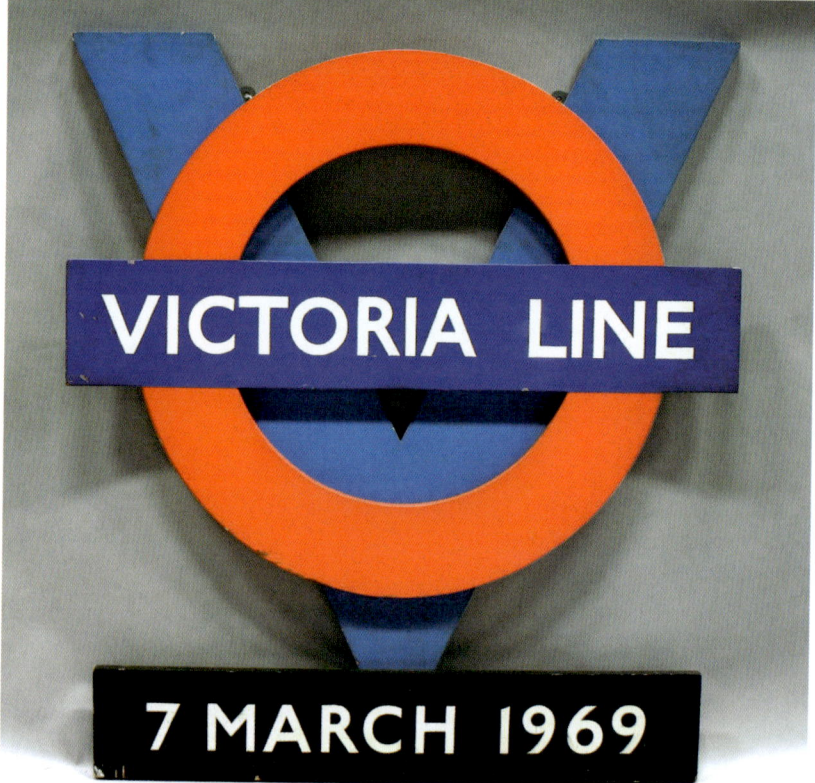

The stripped-down re-design of signage by Misha Black's DRU, still using Johnston's original lettering, is evident in the station frieze (top) and in the headboard for the train that carried Queen Elizabeth II to perform the official opening of the Victoria Line in 1969 (right).

of Johnston. Tracy's conclusions in 1975 were that a total revision of the typeface, retaining the best characteristics of the original, would be the ideal solution, but, failing that, modifications to some of the individual letters to improve readability would be worthwhile. An internal London Transport memo following this report mentions the possibility of ordering custom-made Johnston 'golfballs' – the metal sphere that bore the type – for the electric typewriters in London Transport offices.[63]

Panel poster using Banks & Miles's New Johnston lettering, 1981. The spacing of individual letters has evidently still not been completely mastered in this early example of photo-typesetting for London Transport, but it was soon to improve.

The continued rapid pace of technological change in the printing industry prompted a more radical rethink in the late 1970s. By then the use of private wood and metal type for hand-setting was anachronistic and something of an embarrassment, and the new photo-typesetting systems did not include a version of the Johnston fount. In 1979 the design partnership of Banks & Miles (owned by Colin Banks and John Miles) was given the task of reviewing London Transport's overall publicity, on the back of their successful rebranding of the Royal Mail with a distinctive 'double-line' alphabet. The Banks & Miles report aimed to re-establish a strong coherent visual identity for London Transport, and 'the key issue' they identified was 'whether to abandon or adapt London Transport's iconic Johnston typeface'. The suggestion was that careful updating of the typeface would make it possible to pull London Transport's identity together 'like a ribbon tying up a parcel'. [64]

It appears that the original intention was for a 'somewhat iconoclastic reworking' (as Justin Howes puts it) that would bring Johnston into line with more modern sans serifs such as Helvetica; as David Jury relates, 'it was important to respect the spirit of Johnston rather than adhere mechanically to the construction rules which would have made any further development of the design impossible.' [65]

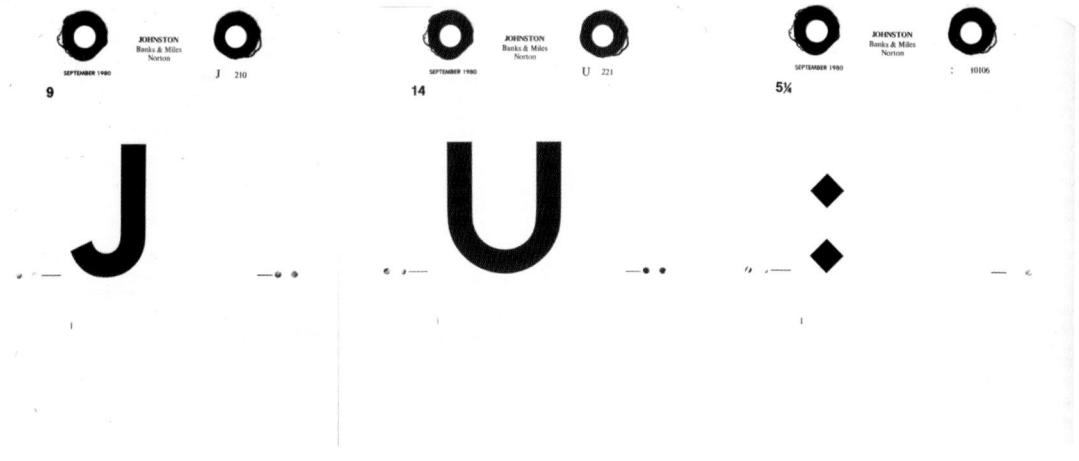

Bromide prints of photo-typeset lettering in New Johnston Medium, 1980.

The detailed redesign job was given to Eiichi Kono, a Japanese optics expert who had retrained as a mature student at the Royal College of Art and who had only recently joined Banks & Miles. The results of Kono's work are what Justin Howes calls a 'scholarly and modest' reinterpretation of the original. Before deploying his optical apparatus on the job, Kono worked in the true Johnston tradition with hand tools – scalpel, Rotring pen and masking tape – to redraft the letters for photo reproduction. Unlike the original typeface, Kono's New Johnston was produced over a relatively short period, and by 1988 comprised nine founts in three weights.[66] Somewhat bathetically it appears that the first display use of New Johnston was on a public information card for tube carriages warning of the severe penalties for assaulting London Transport staff.

The scale of the task was huge. It took twelve years to complete the redesign and implement the New Johnston typeface across all areas of the organisation. But the achievement was impressive: the new founts were suitable for use across all media, so for the first time there was a universal system of lettering for print, display and signage across the entire network.[67]

In 1984 the design agency Henrion Ludlow Schmidt was asked to review London Underground sign design. Their report stressed the value of coherence and recommended the universal application of New Johnston except where heritage signage and decor was to be retained, such as at the listed 1920s and 1930s stations.

A desktop publishing fount, New Johnston Book, was added in 1991 as New Johnston migrated entirely to digital formats. New Johnston and the roundel also spread to parts of the capital not previously reached by Johnston Sans and the bullseye. In 2005, it was decided that the Docklands Light Railway (DLR) should be 'graphically integrated' into the rest of Transport for L, and the original signs in Frutiger and Rockwell were replaced with New Johnston and the roundel.[68] Since 2007, British Rail's 'double-arrow' symbol (designed by Misha Black) and the 1965 Rail Alphabet (by Jock Kinneir and Margaret Calvert) have also been ousted as TfL takes over former British Rail stations in its expanding Overground network. And in 2012 New Johnston could be seen for the first time outside the capital when it was adopted for the Olympic Games directional signage and deployed at games venues in Glasgow, Weymouth, Cardiff and Manchester.

The long struggles with the problems of type manufacture and manual letter spacing are now yesterday's battles. The digital Johnston Sans typeface no longer has any residual physical form. A slipcase containing 3.5-inch New Johnston floppy disks lives on alongside the Banks and Miles photo bromides of New Johnston and a cabinet of Johnston Sans wooden type in the collections of the London Transport Museum – all now technologies of the past. Constant development is a given in Britain's capital city, but the spirit and clarity of Johnston's designs have proved over the last hundred years robust enough to be adaptable to successive waves of technological and social change. Indeed, plans for a second revision of the classic block letter alphabet have been under serious discussion at TfL in recent years. As Johnston's second century dawns, its future as the timeless signature of London seems unassailable.

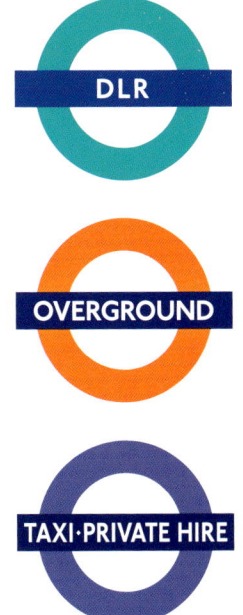

Since 2000, roundels in a range of new colours have been designed for various services falling under the umbrella of Transport for London, a testament to the enduring style and serviceability of Johnston's design.

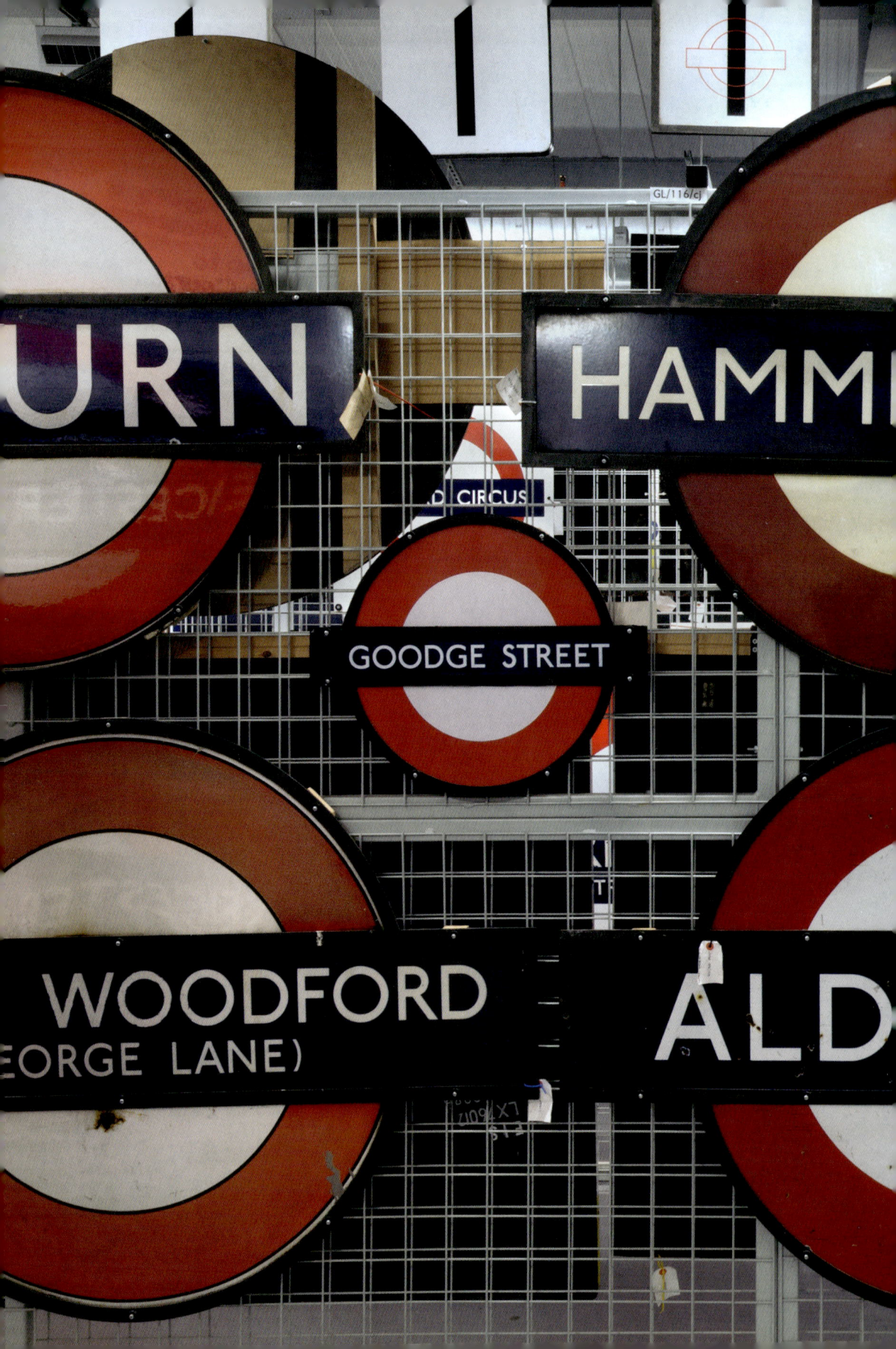

NOTES

1   Frank Pick, 'The Organisation of Transport' in *Journal of the Royal Society of Arts*, Vol. LXXXIV, 3rd January 1936, pp.207-221

2   From a lecture to the Edinburgh branch of the Design and Industries Association, October 1916, quoted in Christian Barman, *Frank Pick: The Man Who Built London Transport* (London, 1979), p.51

3   Quoted in Justin Howes, *Johnston's Underground Type* (London, 2000), p.7. Stanley Morison (1889-1967) was a typographer and historian of printing. Starting in 1913 as editorial assistant on Gerard Meynell's *The Imprint* magazine, he was a typographic consultant to the Monotype Corporation from 1923 to 1967. There he oversaw a significant expansion of Monotype's range of typefaces including the revival of the Baskerville and Bembo faces and the commissioning of Gill Sans. He was also typographic consultant to *The Times* newspaper from 1929 to 1960, and in that capacity developed, with graphic artist Victor Lardent, the Times New Roman typeface.

4   Priscilla Johnston, *Edward Johnston* (second edition, New York, 1976), pp.202-203. Emphases in italics are Edward Johnston's.

5   Priscilla Johnston, p.7. William Graily Hewitt (1864-1952) is regarded by many as second only to Edward Johnston in importance in the early 20th-century revival of calligraphy. Hewitt attended Johnston's classes at the Central School of Arts and Crafts, subsequently

Bullseye station signs with Johnston's block lettering, on display at the London Transport Museum's Acton Depot.

becoming a teacher there and at the Camberwell School of Art. He collaborated with Johnston at Doves Press and wrote the appendix on gilding in Johnston's *Writing & Illuminating & Lettering*, later working with a series of other illuminators and becoming one of the founders of the Society of Scribes and Illuminators in 1921. Hewitt sought to link calligraphy and type design, arguing that type should represent creations of the pen.

6 Justin Howes, p.24

7 Peter Holliday, *Edward Johnston: Master Calligrapher* (London, 2007), pp.13-14

8 Peter Holliday, pp.17-18

9 Peter Holliday, p.16

10 Priscilla Johnston, pp.282-284

11 Peter Holliday, p.15

12 Coincidentally, as a boy Frank Pick was also fascinated by, and gave presents of, miniature toys: *see* Christian Barman, p.16. Many of Johnston's gadgets and toys still survive in the care of Ditchling Museum of Art and Craft, alongside other significant Johnston artefacts, including his writing desk.

13 Bernard Newdigate, writing in *The Imprint*, 17th February 1913, quoted in Justin Howes, p.8

14 Edward Johnston in 1934 and 1930 respectively, quoted in Justin Howes, p.8

15 Peter Holliday, p.1

16 Peter Holliday, p.4

17 Ewan Clayton, *Edward Johnston: Lettering and Life* (Ditchling Museum, 2007), p.11

18 Priscilla Johnston, quoted in Peter Holliday, p.367

19 Peter Holliday, p.372

20 London Transport Museum Frank Pick Collection PB49: Frank Pick, 'The Meaning and Purpose of Design', lecture notes, 19th June 1933

21 Priscilla Johnston, p.31

22 Priscilla Johnston, p.41

23 Ewan Clayton, p.12

24 Priscilla Johnston, pp.224, 161-2

25 Ewan Clayton, p.13

26 William Harrison Cowlishaw (1869–1957), a follower of William Morris, was commissioned after the end of the First World War by the Imperial (now Commonwealth) War Graves Commission to design memorials and cemetery layouts in Flanders and France. His work includes the Pozières Memorial in the Somme and the Prowse Point, Rifle House and Devonshire cemeteries around Ypres. It was whilst working at the Commission that he met Charles Holden.

27 Sydney Carlyle Cockerell (1867-1962) was, from 1908 to 1937, the director of the Fitzwilliam Museum in Cambridge. He built up the museum's collections of private-press books and manuscripts, prints, drawings, fine art and antiquities, raised funds for building extensions, set up the first museum 'Friends' scheme in Britain and introduced Sunday opening. He was knighted in 1934. A lifelong friend of Edward Johnston, he encouraged Johnston's youngest daughter Priscilla to write her father's biography for which Cockerell wrote the foreword.

28 Ewan Clayton, p.13

29 Priscilla Johnston, p.101, p.204

30 Noel Rooke (1881–1953) had been employed by William Lethaby in 1899 to make drawings of the Chapter House at Westminster Abbey, and then joined the Central School of Arts and Crafts as a student. In 1905 Rooke became a teacher of book illustration at the Central School, and from 1914 until 1946 was head of the School of Book Production. Rooke applied Johnston's teaching (to wood engraving) that the form of a letter should be determined by the tool, and was a major influence in reviving the practice of wood engraving in the 20th century, helping to found the Society of Wood Engravers in 1920. He also later designed posters for the Underground. Thomas James Cobden-Sanderson (1840-1922), a friend of William Morris, abandoned a career in law in the mid 1880s to open a bookbinding workshop. He is credited with suggesting the name 'Arts and Crafts Exhibition Society' which came to stand for all those associated with Morris. His Doves Bindery in Hammersmith was established in 1893, named after a nearby pub, and by 1900 he had established the Doves

Press in partnership with another friend of William Morris, Emery Walker (1851-1933). Walker oversaw the creation of a typeface for Doves Press, but the partnership dissolved in acrimony after 1909. On final closure of the press in 1916, Cobden-Sanderson threw the Doves type along with its punches and matrices off Hammersmith Bridge into the Thames to deny it to Walker. (Some pieces of type were recovered from the riverbed in 2015.) Percy Smith (1882-1948) became a painter, etcher, calligrapher and book designer, publishing his textbook *Civic and Memorial Lettering* in 1946. On his marriage to the research biologist Marion Delf in 1928 he changed his name to Percy Delf Smith. Leslie MacDonald (Max) Gill (1884-1947), a younger brother of Eric Gill (1882-1940), became a noted graphic designer, cartographer, artist and architect. His humorous and popular 'Wonderground Map' of 1914, commissioned by Frank Pick, established his reputation; he went on to design the standard upper case lettering used on headstones and war memorials by the Imperial War Graves Commission. Following his divorce in 1946 he married his long-standing lover and god-daughter, Priscilla Johnston.

31 Priscilla Johnston, p.101, p.204
32 Told to Peyton Skipwith by Edward Bawden in the 1980s, as quoted in Oliver Green, *Frank Pick's London* (London, 2013), p.51. Edward Bawden (1903-1989) went on to become a noted painter, illustrator and graphic artist. It was at the Royal College that Bawden met his fellow student and future collaborator, Eric Ravilious (1903-42): the pair were described by their teacher, Paul Nash, as 'an extraordinary outbreak of talent'. From the 1930s Bawden produced many posters for clients such as Shell-Mex, Imperial Airways and London Transport, and then served as an official war artist from 1939-1945. Surviving post-war public works by Bawden include *Ferry Across the River Lea* – a tile mural at Tottenham Hale underground station, and the silhouette of Queen Victoria used at Victoria underground station.
33 Priscilla Johnston, p.114
34 Douglas Clark Pepler (1878-1951) was known as Hilary after his conversion to Roman Catholicism in 1917.
35 Priscilla Johnston, p.225

NOTES

36 Priscilla Johnston, p.225
37 Ewan Clayton, p.17
38 Edward Johnston lecture, 'Signwriting', at Leicester School of Art, 28th September 1906, quoted in Justin Howes, p.17
39 Quoted in Justin Howes, pp.17-18
40 Justin Howes, p.19
41 Oliver Green, p.47. *See also* Barman, pp.37-38
42 As recalled by Walter Gott and quoted in Barman, pp.28-29
43 As an illustration of how closely intertwined were the various strands of Johnston's life, Frank Pick and Douglas Pepler were educated in York at exactly the same time: Pick at St Peter's School and Pepler at the Quaker Bootham School, only 500 yards away. At Bootham, Pepler seems to have befriended members of the Meynell family. Gerard Tuke Meynell was a descendant of the Tuke family of York who sold their cocoa business in that city to their fellow Quakers the Rowntrees, and their London tea business to their relatives the Mennells (the variants 'Mennell' and 'Meynell' were both used by the family.) On leaving school, Pepler is known to have spent time in the tea trade in London, and to have initially shared a house with Harry Mennell (of the Quaker branch of the family). Through Harry he became very friendly with the children of Wilfrid and Alice Meynell (the Catholic branch) who were Gerard's brother and sister-in-law.
44 Christian Barman, p.43
45 Priscilla Johnston, p.201
46 This section draws heavily on Justin Howes, pp.28-26.
47 Nikolaus Pevsner, 'Patient Progress – The Life Work of Frank Pick' in *Architectural Review*, 92:548 (August 1942), p.32
48 Priscilla Johnston, pp.201-202
49 Priscilla Johnston, p.265
50 Justin Howes, p.60
51 Priscilla Johnston, pp.204-205; Barman, pp.45-46
52 Priscilla Johnston, p.204
53 Justin Howes, p.50
54 Justin Howes, p.57
55 Justin Howes, pp.57-59

56 Justin Howes, p.59, note 2. The LT Museum inventory number for the blotter is 2000/8000.

57 Percy J. Delf Smith, *Civic and Memorial Lettering* (London, 1946), pp.28-29

58 Mark Ovenden, *London Underground by Design* (London, 2013), pp.151, 164-165

59 Mark Ovenden, p.155

60 Brian Webb, 'The Roller Coaster Ride: London Transport Posters since 1945' in David Bownes & Oliver Green (ed.), *London Transport Posters – A Century of Art and Design* (London, 2008), p.190

61 David Lawrence, *A Logo For London* (second edition, London, 2013), p.88

62 David Lawrence, p.107

63 'Aide-Memoire: The Tracy/Johnston Alphabet 31 Oct 1975' – notes of a meeting on 29th October 1975 between 'the Chairman, Mr Robbins, Walter Tracy and I [assumed to be Bryce Beaumont, Publicity Officer]' in LT Museum Object File 1985/56

64 Brian Webb, p.201

65 Justin Howes, p.65; David Jury, *About Face, Reviving the Rules of Typography* (Mies, Switzerland, 2004) pp.60-61

66 For a detailed account of the redesign work, see Eiichi Kono, 'New Johnston' in *Pen to Printer* (Edward Johnston Foundation, 2003), http://www.ejf.org.uk/Resources/ekono.pdf, accessed 1st February 2016

67 Brian Webb, p.201

68 Mark Ovenden, p.254

Opposite and on pages 88 and 90 Station signs on display at the London Transport Museum's Acton Depot.

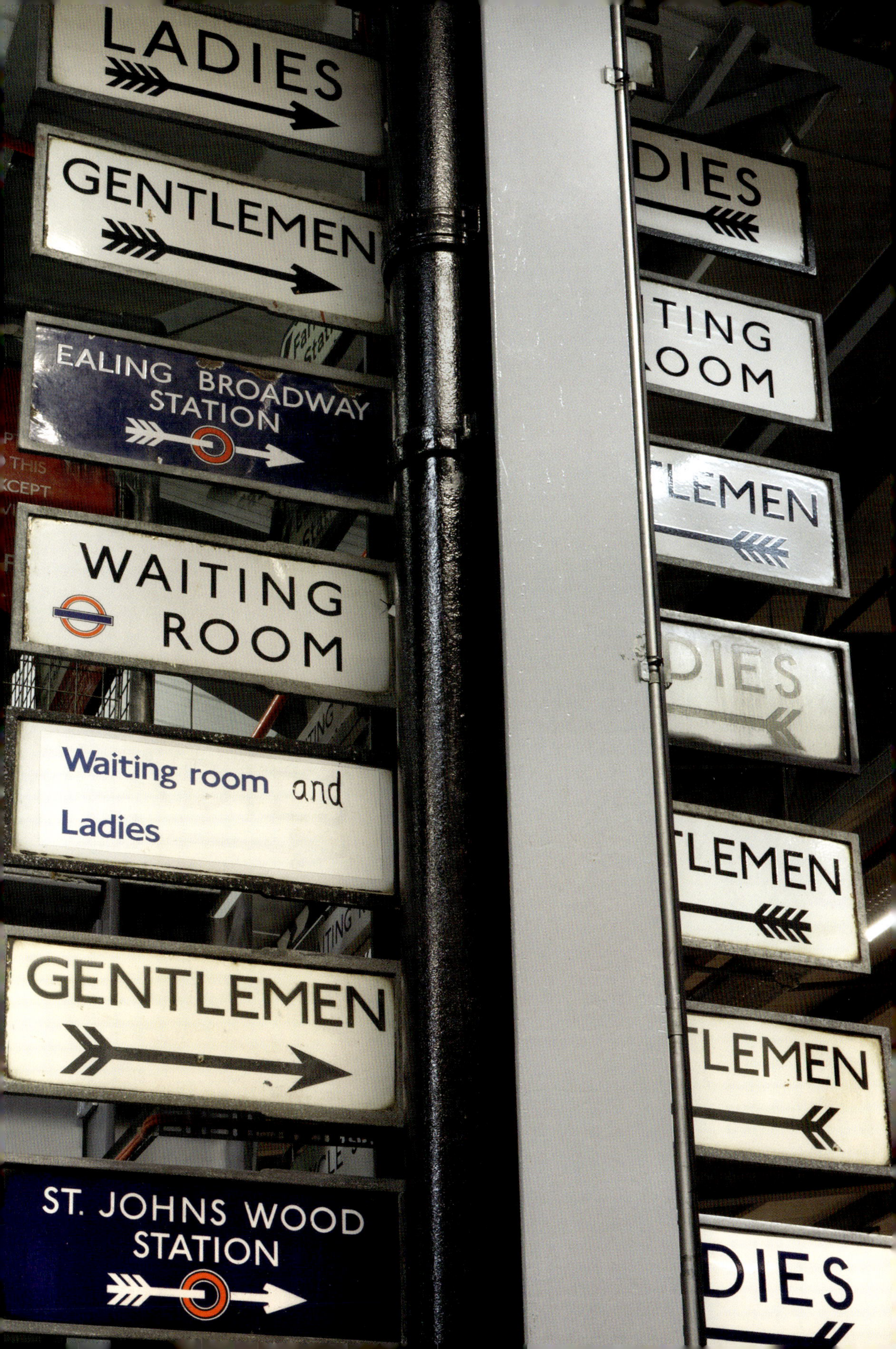

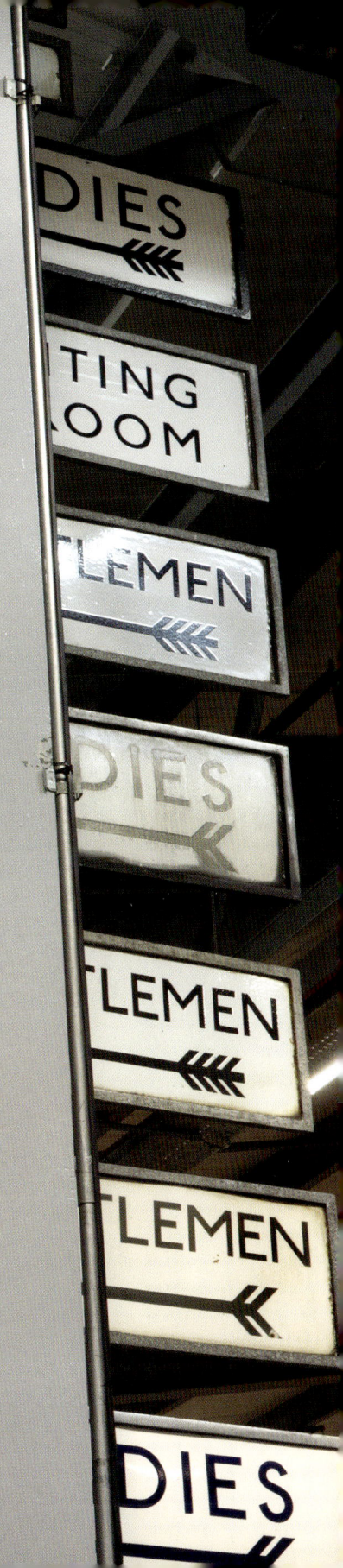

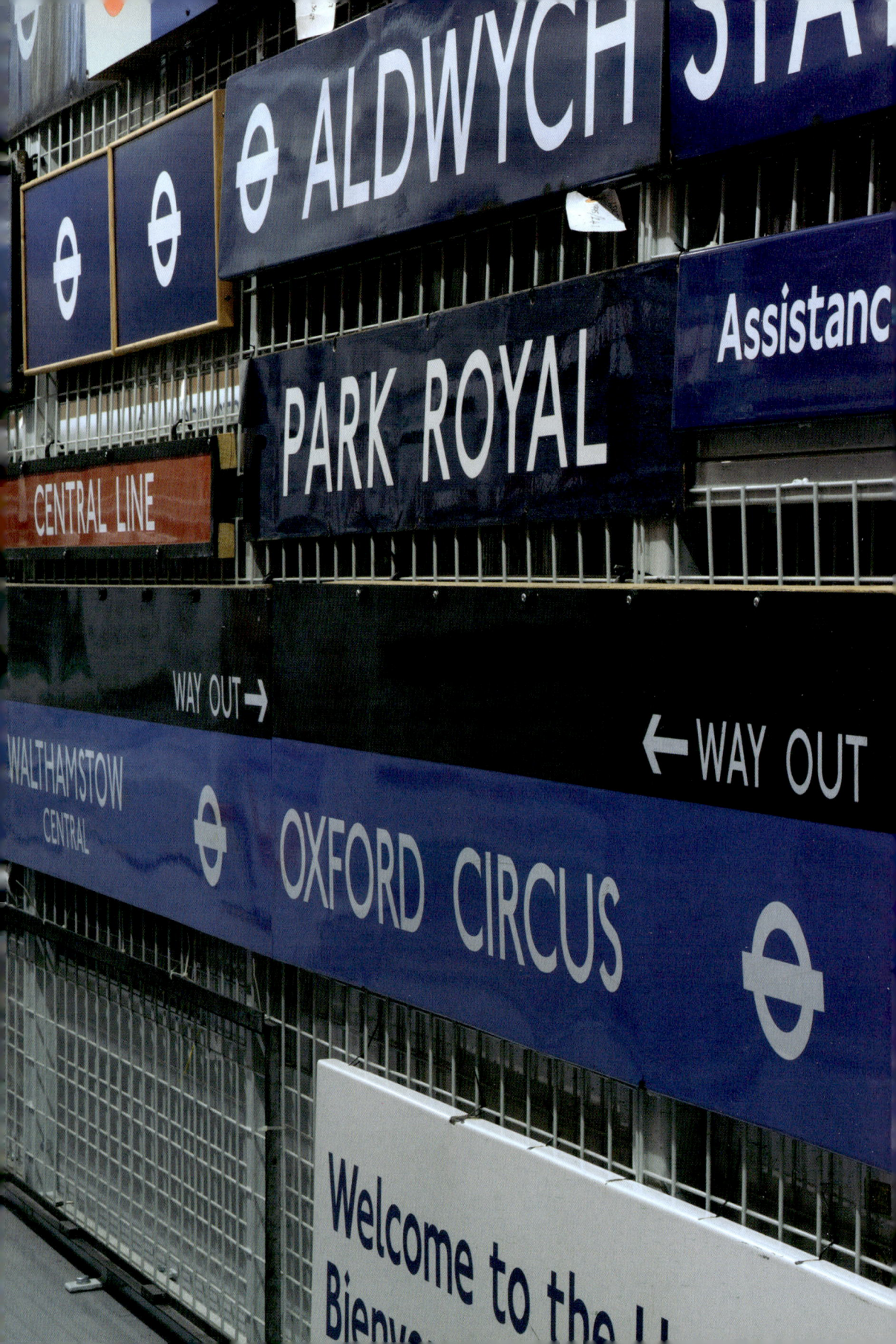

BIBLIOGRAPHY & SUGGESTIONS FOR FURTHER READING

Bownes, David & Green, Oliver (ed.), *London Transport Posters – A Century of Art and Design*, Lund Humphries/London Transport Museum, London, 2008

Clayton, Ewan, *Edward Johnston: Lettering & Life*, exhibition catalogue, Ditchling Museum of Art and Craft, East Sussex, 2007

Clayton, Ewan, *The Golden Thread: The Story of Writing*, Atlantic Books, London, 2013

Garfield, Simon, *Just My Type*, Profile Books, London, 2010

Green, Oliver, *Frank Pick's London*, V&A Publishing, London 2013

Holliday, Peter, *Edward Johnston: Master Calligrapher*, Oak Knoll Press & the British Library, New Castle (Delaware) & London, 2007

Howes, Justin, *Johnston's Underground Type*, Capital Transport Publishing, Middlesex, 2000

Johnston, Edward, *Writing & Illuminating & Lettering*, Pitman, London, 1906; reprinted by A. & C. Black, London, 1983

Johnston, Priscilla, *Edward Johnston*, Faber & Faber, London, 1959; second edition, Pentalic Corporation, New York, 1976

Kono, Eiichi, 'New Johnston' in *Pen to Printer*, Edward Johnston Foundation, 2003; http://www.ejf.org.uk/Resources/ekono.pdf, accessed 1 Feb 2016

Jury, David, *About Face, Reviving the Rules of Typography*, Rotovision, Brighton, 2004

Lawrence, David, *A Logo For London*, Laurence King Publishing/London Transport Museum, London, 2013

Loxley, Simon, *Type: The Secret History of Letters*, I. B. Tauris & Co., London & New York, 2004

MacCarthy, Fiona, *Eric Gill*, Faber & Faber, London, 1989

Millington, Roy, *Stephenson Blake, The Last of the Old English Typefounders*, Oak Knoll Press & the British Library, New Castle (Delaware) & London, 2002

Ovenden, Mark, *London Underground By Design*, Penguin Books, London, 2013

Pevsner, Nikolaus, 'Patient Progress – The Life Work of Frank Pick' in *The Architectural Review* 92:548, London, August 1942, pp.31–48

Smith, Percy Delf, *Civic and Memorial Lettering*, A. & C. Black, London, 1946

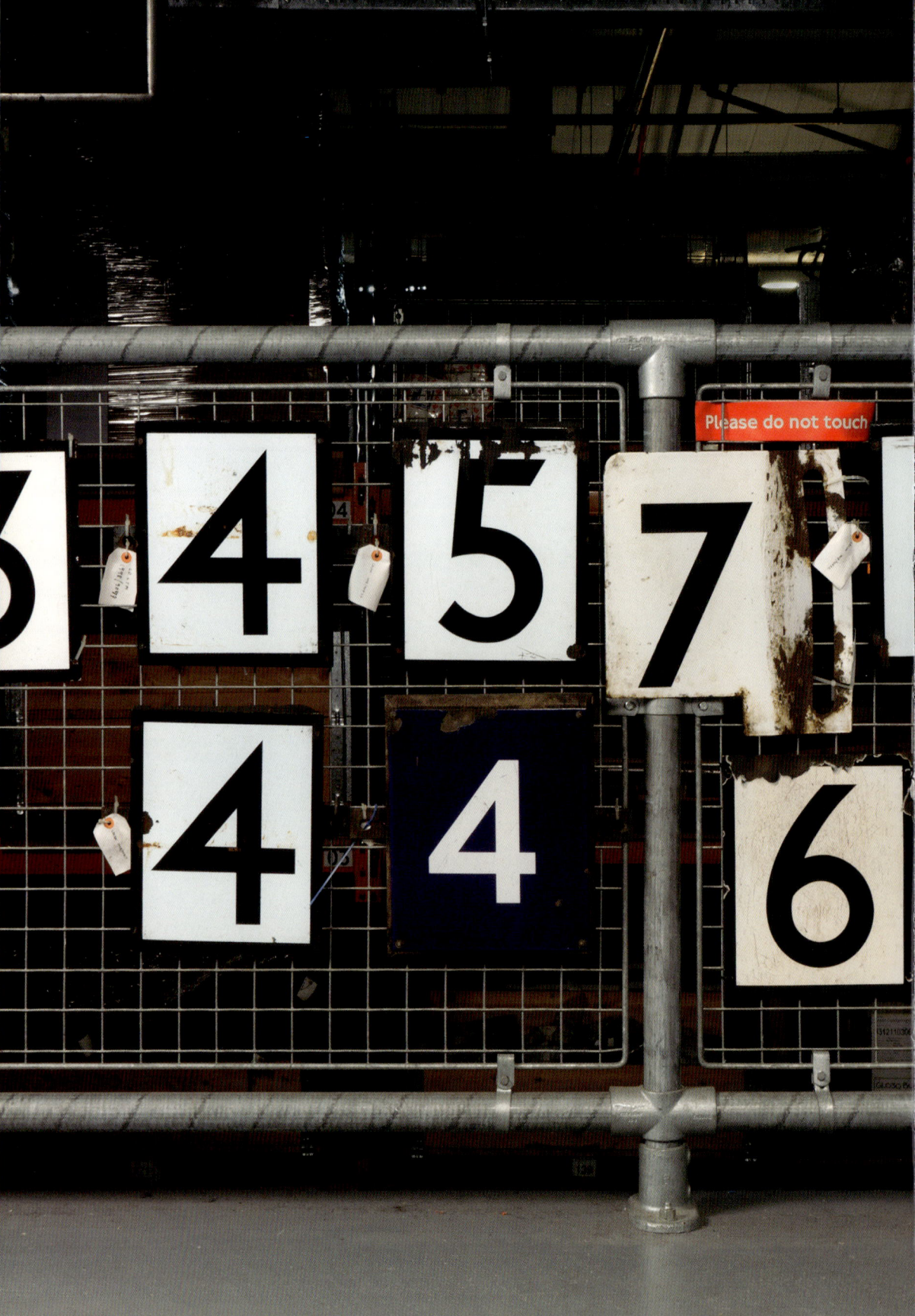

INDEX

Page numbers in italic indicate references in captions

About Face, Reviving the Rules of Typography (Howes) 86
Aerial World, The 15
Aldenham Bus Overhaul Works 42
Alice in Wonderland 33
Arazaty, The
Architectural Review, The 85
Artist, The 29
Arts and Crafts Exhibition 1916 58
Arts and Crafts Exhibition Society 14, 41, 83
Arts and Crafts Movement 8, 11, 14, 15, 22, 39, 46
Ashfield, Lord (aka Albert Stanley) 46, 48, *48*, 50, 61, 66, *67*, 71, 74
Atlantic 23, 30
Aunt Buxton 25

Baker Street and Waterloo Railway 46
Balham, London 23
Banks, Colin 77
Banks & Miles 77, *77*, 78
Barclays 21
Barman, Christian 81, 82, 85
Baskerville typeface 81
Bawden, Edward 33, 84
Beaumont, Bryce 86
Bembo typeface *81*
Bethnal Green station 53
Black, Misha 75, *76*, 79
Bownes, David 86
British Columbia 27, *27*, 28
British Empire Exhibition 1924-25 60
British Museum Library 14, 30

British Rail 79
Broadway, 55, London 69
bullseye logotype 16, 37, 46, 60, 71, 74, 75, 79, *81*
Burlington House, Piccadilly 58
Buxton family 21

Calvert, Margaret 79
Camberwell School of Art 82
Canada 27
Cardiff 79
Carr-Edwards Report 53, 71, *71*, 74
Carr, Henry 64, 71, 74
Central School of Arts and Crafts 30, 35, 45, 81, 83
Central St Martins College and the Crafts Study Centre 33
Charing Cross, Euston and Hampstead Railway 46
Chicago 27
Civic and Memorial Lettering (Delf Smith) 69, 84, 86
Clayton, Ewan 19, 24, 28, 30, 41, 82, 83, 85
Cobden-Sanderson, Thomas James 33, 35, 36, 39, 83, 84
Cockerell, Sydney Carlyle 30, 31, 83
Cowlishaw, William Harrison (Harry) 28, 29, 30, 83
Craig, Edward Gordon 36
Cranach Press 36, *36*
Cribb, Joseph 42

Delf, Marion 84
Delf Smith, Percy 33, 69, *69*, 84, 86
Design and Industries Association (DIA) 45, 46, 81
Design Research Unit (DRU) 75, *76*
Deutscher Werkbund (German Association of Craftsmen) 46
Devonshire war cemetery 83
DIA see Design and Industries Association
District Line 50
District Railway 49, 51
Ditchling 7, 17, *38*, 39, 40, 41, 42
Ditchling Common 40
Ditchling Museum of Art and Craft 42, 82
Docklands Light Railway (DLR) 79
Douglas, Alice see Johnston, Alice
Douglas, Margaret (aka Aunty Maggie)
Doves Bindery 83
Doves Press 35, *35*, 36, 82, 84

Edinburgh 81
Edinburgh University 26
Edwards, W. P. N. 71
Edward Johnston: Lettering and Life (Clayton) 82
Edward Johnston: Master Calligrapher (Holliday) 82
Elliott, Sir John 74
England 23, 24, 28
England, Eric 8
Essex 26
Essex County Council 25

Fabian Society 39
Ferry Across the River Lea 84

91

Fife 21
Finchley East station 8
First World War 61, 83
Fitzwilliam Museum 83
Flanders 83
France 83
Franklin Gothic 45
Frank Pick: The Man Who Built London Transport (Barman) 81
Frank Pick's London (Green) 84
Frutiger typeface 79
Fry, Elizabeth (*née* Gurney) 21

Game, The 40, 41
German Association of Craftsmen *see* Deutscher Werkbund
Germany 45
Gibb, George 46
Gill, Eric 22, 33, 35, 38, 39, 40, 41, *41*, 42, 45, 53, *53*, 54, 64, 84
Gill, Leslie MacDonald (Max) 33, 84
Gill Sans typeface 33, 58, 75
Ginnett, Louis 7
Ginnett, Mary 7
Glasgow 79
Gott, Walter 86
Gray's Inn Road 29, No. 4, 38
Great Northern, Piccadilly and Brompton Railway 46
Great War *see* First World War
Green, Oliver 5, 84, 85, 86
Green Line 62
Green Park station 60
Greenwich cable car 75
Grieg, Greta *see* Johnston, Greta
Guide Book of Ditchling 38
Guild of St Joseph and St Dominic 40
Gurney, Elizabeth *see* Fry, Elizabeth
Gurney family 21

Halletts Farm 40, 54
Hammersmith 58, 83
Hammersmith Bridge 84
Hammersmith Terrace, No. 3 38
Hampstead 23
Hanbury family 21
Harrison 27
Hassall, John 48
Hastings 23
Hawkes, Violet 33
Helvetica typeface 77
Henrion Ludlow Schmidt 78
Hewitt, William Graily 13, 33, 81, 82
High Sheriff of Essex 22
Holden, Charles 28, 60, *60*, 69, 83
Holliday, Peter 14, 15, 17, 18, 22, 82
Howes, Justin 45, 61, 64, 66, 77, 78, 81, 82, 85, 86
Hugh, Bernhard 48
Hutchison, Harold 74, 75

Ideal Book or Book Beautiful, The 35, 36
Imperial Airways 84
Imperial (now Commonwealth) War Graves Commission 83, 84
Imprint, The magazine 36, *37*, 81, 82
India 2

Johnston Sans typeface 7, *11*, 16, 58, 59, 60, 75, 79
Johnston, Ada 23, 24
Johnston, Alice (*née* Douglas) 23, 25, 26
Johnston, Andrew (Edward Johnston's brother) 22, 25
Johnston, Andrew (Edward Johnston's grandson) 27
Johnston, Andrew (Edward Johnston's uncle) 21, 25, 26, 27
Johnston, Fowell Buxton 21, 22, 23, 26
Johnston, Greta (*née* Grieg) 39, 40, 42
Johnston, Miles 23, 26, 39
Johnston, Olof 23
Johnston, Priscilla 11, 14, *15*, 21, 22, 23, 24, 27, 29, 40, 56, 63, 81, 82, 83, 84, 85
Johnston's Underground Type (Howes) 81
Jury, David 77, 86

Kessler, Count Harry 36, *36*, 45
Kettelred 23
Kinneir, Jock 79
Kippen 18
Kono, Eiichi 78, 86

Lawrence, David 62, 86
Lessons in the Art of Illumination (Loftie) 25
Lethaby, William 29, 30, 33, 38, 83
Leicester School of Art 85
Lewisham 23
Lincoln's Inn, London 12, 17, 38
Lincolnshire 46
Listener, The 18
Loftie, William John 25
Logo For London, A 86
London 12, 23, 25, 28, 29, 38, 41, 48, 51, 63, 79, 85
London County Council (LCC) 29
–Technical Education Board of 29
London Electric Railways 12
London General Omnibus Company 15, *47*, 62
London North Eastern Railway 47
London Passenger Transport Board (LPTB) 41, 46, 61, 66

INDEX

London Transport Museum 66, 69, 79
–Acton Depot 81, 86
London Transport Posters – A Century of Art and Design 86
London Underground by Design 86

MacInnes family 38
MacInnes, Neil 26, *27*, 28
MacInness, Dora 38
MacRae family 28, 29
MacRae, Mollie 29
Magnificat 25
Manchester 79
Mason, J. H. 36
Men & Women (Browning) 35
Mennell, Harry 85
Metropolitan District Railway 45, 46, *47*, 50
Metropolitan Railway 48, *49*
Meynell, Alice 85
Meynell, Gerard Tuke 22, 36, 37, 53, 54, 66, 81, 85
Meynell, Wilfrid 85
Meynell family 85
Middle East 19
Miles, John 77
Mill Book, The (Johnston) 39
Monotype Corporation 33, 58, 81
Monument station *48*
Morison, Stanley 11, 13, 36, 81
Morris, William 14, 29, 30, 35, 83, 84
Morrow, George *59*
'Mussel Andrew' *18*
Muthesius, Herman 46

Nash, Paul 84
New Broad Street, London EC4 25
New Cross, London 26
Newdigate, Bernard 15, 82

New Johnston typeface 78, *78*, 79
New Works Programme 71
New York 27
Norfolk 21
North Berwick 38
North Eastern Railway 46
Northern City Line *42*
Northern Line *42*

Okehampton 23
Olympic Games 2012 79
Ovenden, Mark *45*, 86
Overground 75, 79

Pen to Printer 86
Pepler, David 39
Pepler, Douglas 38, 39, *39*, 40, 41, *42*, 45, 54, 84, 85
Pevsner, Nikolaus 56, 85
Piccadilly *60*
Piccadilly Line *17*, 69
Piccadilly Railway *17*
Pick, Frank 7, 11, 22, 37, 41, 42, 46, *46*, *47*, 50, 51, *51*, 53, *53*, 54, *54*, 61, *61*, 62, 64, 66, *67*, 82, 84
Plymouth 23
Portland Stone *60*
Pozières Memorial 83
Prime Minister 17
Primrose Hill, London 23
Prince of Wales 25
Prowse Point war cemetery 83

Quaker 21, 22, 39
Quaker Bootham School, York 85
Queen Elizabeth II 76

Rail Alphabet typeface 79
Ramsey Psalter 14
Ravilious, Eric 84
Registered Designer for Industry 14
Renaissance 19

Rennyhill 21
Rifle House war cemetery 83
Robert De Little of York 56
Robbins, Mr 86
Rockwell typeface 79
Roman Catholicism 84
Rome 53
Rooke, Noel 33, *35*, 45, 83
Rowntrees 85
Royal College of Art, London 31, 33, *33*, 41, 78, 84
Royal Mail 77
Royal Society of Arts 14

St Dominic's Press 38
St James Park station 53
St Peter's School, York 85
Salt Lake City 27
Salt Spring Island 27, *28*, 28
San José 21
Schleger, Hans (aka 'Zero') 70, 71, 74
Scotland 23
Seattle 27
Second World War 53, 74
Shakespeare, William 7
Shakespeare's Sonnets 35
Sharland, Charles *48*
Shaw, Norman 29
Shell-Mex 84
Shepherd's Bush, London *58*
Shoreditch station *47*
Skipwith, Peyton 84
Smith, Percy *see* Delf Smith, Percy
Society of Scribes and Illuminators 82
Society of Wood Engravers 83
Society for the Protection of Ancient Buildings 29
Somme 83
South America 22
South Norwood, London 23
Standard Alphabet 7, 11, *60*, *63*
Standard Block Lettering 37

93

Standard Signs manual 71
Stanley, Albert *see* Ashfield, Lord 46, *48*, 50
Stations of the Cross 54
Stephenson Blake of Sheffield 56
Stirlingshire 18
Sudbury Town station 69
Sussex 18

Thames, river 84
3rd Dragoon Guards 22
Torquay *18*, 23
Tottenham Hale station 84
Tracy, Walter 75, 76, 86
Trajan's Column, Rome 14, 53
Tragedie of Hamlet Prince of Denmark 36
Transport for London (TfL) 69, 74, 75, *79*, 79
Tuke family 85
Turnham Green, London 23

Underground Electric Railways Group of London (UERL) 11, 16, 28, 37, 46, *46*, *47*, 48, 56, 58, *59*, 69
Underground Group 7, 41, 62, 64
Unilever 74
Univers typeface 75
Upper Norwood, London 23
Uruguay 21, 23, 26
USA 27

Ventnor 23
Verderer of Epping Forest 22
Victoria, Queen 84
Victoria Line 75, *76*
Victoria underground station 84

Walker, Emery 35, 39, 84
Waterlows *11*
Webb, Brian 74, 86
Weimar 36

Wembley 60
Westminster station *50*
Westminster Abbey, Chapter House at 83
Westminster Bridge station *50*
Westminster Cathedral 54
Westminster Press 36, 37
Weymouth 79
Who's Who 11
W. H. Smith & Sons 53, *53*
Wilberforce, William 21
Wimbledon 58
Wonderground Map 84
Woodford 26
Writing & Illuminating & Lettering (Johnston) 13, 14, 18, *19*, *20*, 35, 82

York 46, 51, 85
Young Men's Christian Association (YMCA) 61
– YMCA Hut Day *47*
Ypres 83

'Zero' *see* Schleger, Hans

AUTHOR'S ACKNOWLEDGEMENTS

I would like to express my appreciation to everyone below for their invaluable help whilst writing this modest tribute to the genius of Edward Johnston. My apologies to anyone whom I have inadvertently omitted from this list.

Mark Eastment, Brian Webb and Jill Hollis (my editor) for making this book a reality.

All my former London Transport Museum colleagues including Sam Clift, Valia Lamprou, Simon Murphy, Chris Nix, Laura Sleath, Tom Walker, Caroline Warhurst and Louise White; and especially the London Transport Museum 'Johnston Journeys' volunteer team for their enthusiasm and commitment, Sam Mullins for writing the foreword, Marilyn Greene for her sterling work on the illustrations, and Elizabeth Scott for championing the book and her kindness and understanding.

Being able to draw on the knowledge and erudition of the wider Johnstonian community was a great privilege and I am grateful to Andrew and Angela Johnston; Eiichi Kono; Gerald Fleuss and Patricia Gidney (Edward Johnston Foundation), Judy Willcocks, Phil Baines and Catherine Dixon (Central Saint Martins – UAL); Nathaniel Hepburn and Donna Steele (Ditchling Museum of Art & Craft); Oliver Green and David Lawrence.

And finally thanks to my old friends Margaret Lamb and Andrew Smith for their five-star hospitality on my London research trips, and to my wife Judy Burg for her patience, encouragement, and endless cups of coffee.

Richard Taylor
York, March 2016